Taiwan Travel Guide: A Journey of Heritage and Beauty.

Kendrick Owens

TABLE OF CONTENTS

Introduction

Welcome to the captivating island of Taiwan, where modern marvels harmoniously coexist with ancient traditions, creating a destination that enchants and beguiles all who visit. Nestled in the heart of East Asia, Taiwan is a treasure trove of diverse landscapes, rich history, delectable cuisine, and warm-hearted people. This travel guide is your passport to uncovering the myriad wonders that await you on this island gem.

Taiwan is a place where bustling metropolises seamlessly blend with serene countryside, and where traditional temples stand in the shadow of modern skyscrapers. From the vibrant night markets of Taipei to the serene shores of Sun Moon Lake, every corner of Taiwan tells a unique story, narrated by its history, culture, and people.

Steeped in history, Taiwan boasts a heritage that has been shaped by indigenous cultures, colonial influences, and waves of migration. Ancient temples dedicated to various deities stand as symbols of devotion and tradition, while vibrant festivals bring the island to life with colorful parades, elaborate processions, and cultural performances.

Prepare your taste buds for a journey through one of Asia's most renowned culinary landscapes. Taiwan's street food scene is legendary, with night markets offering a tantalizing array of dishes, from the iconic stinky tofu to mouthwatering xiao long bao (soup dumplings). Explore the lively food stalls, traditional teahouses, and innovative restaurants that make Taiwan a paradise for food enthusiasts.

From the dramatic peaks of Taroko Gorge to the idyllic beaches of Kenting, Taiwan's natural beauty is a canvas of diversity. Hikers will find themselves immersed in lush forests, while adventure seekers can conquer the towering Alishan mountain range. On the east coast, the Pacific Ocean crashes against rugged cliffs, creating a mesmerizing coastal panorama.

While Taiwan's landscapes and attractions are undeniably captivating, it's the warmth and hospitality of its people that truly leave an indelible mark. Known for their friendliness and helpfulness, the Taiwanese locals are always eager to share their culture, stories, and recommendations, making your journey even more enriching.

This comprehensive Taiwan travel guide is your trusted companion as you embark on this unforgettable adventure. Whether you're a solo traveler, a family exploring with children, or a couple seeking romantic escapes, you'll find tailored recommendations, insider tips, and practical advice to make the most of your time in Taiwan.

From the bustling urban hubs of Taipei and Kaohsiung to the tranquil beauty of the East Rift Valley and the off-the-beaten-path treasures waiting to be discovered, let this guide be your compass as you navigate Taiwan's unique blend of past and present, nature and culture, tradition and innovation. Get ready to immerse yourself in the essence of Taiwan – a land that promises awe, inspiration, and the magic of discovery at every turn.

Chapter 1. About Taiwan

- *Geographical Overview*

Nestled off the southeastern coast of China, Taiwan emerges as a captivating island nation that boasts a geographical diversity as mesmerizing as its cultural tapestry. With its lush landscapes, towering peaks, serene lakes, and stunning coastlines, Taiwan's geography is a testament to nature's artistry. As you embark on your journey through this island paradise, let's explore the key geographical features that define Taiwan's allure.

1. Rugged Mountain Ranges

Central Taiwan is dominated by a spine of rugged mountain ranges that stretch from the north to the south, earning the island its nickname, "Ilha Formosa," or "Beautiful Island." The Central Mountain Range, flanked by peaks that often exceed 10,000 feet, is a paradise for hikers and nature enthusiasts. Alishan's misty forests and the dramatic cliffs of Taroko Gorge exemplify the raw beauty of Taiwan's topography.

2. Verdant Valleys and Plains

Nestled between the mountainous terrain, Taiwan's valleys and plains offer a refreshing contrast. The fertile lands of the western plains are a patchwork of rice paddies, tea plantations, and vibrant cities. The sun-drenched Changhua and Chiayi plains are the heart of Taiwan's agricultural activity, while the Yilan Plain to the northeast is renowned for its picturesque landscapes.

3. Coastal Splendor

Taiwan's coastline is a varied masterpiece that ranges from rugged cliffs to sandy shores. The East Coast, lapped by the Pacific Ocean, is a dramatic blend of soaring cliffs, crashing waves, and serene fishing villages. The contrasting West Coast is dotted with bustling cities, charming fishing ports, and tranquil beaches perfect for relaxation and water sports.

4. Enchanting Lakes and Reservoirs

Nestled amid the verdant mountains are Taiwan's enchanting lakes and reservoirs. Sun Moon Lake, with its reflective waters surrounded by lush forests, is a symbol of tranquility. Additionally, the serene vistas of Qingjing's Green Green Grasslands and the secluded beauty of Lugu Lake offer a glimpse into Taiwan's quieter, more contemplative side.

5. Volcanic Treasures

Taiwan's geological history has gifted the island with volcanic wonders. Yangmingshan National Park, located just outside Taipei, showcases volcanic landscapes, hot springs, and sulfur vents. The active hot springs in Beitou and the mud springs of Wulai are testament to the island's geothermal activity.

6. Offshore Islands

Beyond the main island, Taiwan's maritime realm extends to several smaller islands. The Penghu Archipelago is renowned for its coral reefs and picturesque landscapes, while the orchid island of Lanyu offers a unique blend of indigenous culture and natural beauty. Kinmen and Matsu, situated close to China's coast, add historical depth to Taiwan's story.

7. Climate Variability

Taiwan's geography also influences its climate, creating diverse weather patterns across the island.

The northern regions experience distinct seasons, while the southern parts enjoy a more tropical climate. The island's diverse weather can range from mist-shrouded mountains to balmy beaches, providing a dynamic backdrop for your exploration.

As you traverse Taiwan's varied landscapes, each step reveals a new facet of the island's geographic splendor. From the soaring peaks to the tranquil lakes, and from the bustling cityscapes to the untouched offshore gems, Taiwan's geography is an open invitation to uncover its countless treasures. Embrace the enchanting interplay between nature and culture as you embark on a journey that transcends the boundaries of time and place.

- Historical and Cultural Background

Taiwan's historical and cultural narrative is a captivating tapestry woven with influences from indigenous cultures, Chinese traditions, colonial powers, and more. This island's story is one of resilience, transformation, and the emergence of a unique identity that blends the old and the new, the traditional and the modern.

Indigenous Roots

Long before the arrival of other cultures, Taiwan was home to a vibrant array of indigenous peoples, collectively known as the Austronesian tribes. These indigenous groups, each with their own languages, customs, and belief systems, are the original inhabitants of the island and continue to play an integral role in Taiwan's cultural fabric.

Colonial Eras

The 17th century marked the beginning of external influences on Taiwan. The island became a Dutch colony, followed by Spanish rule, and later, Ming Dynasty refugees and Qing Dynasty influence. It was during the Qing Dynasty's rule that Chinese migration to Taiwan increased, leading to the blending of Han Chinese culture with the existing indigenous cultures.

Japanese Occupation

Taiwan's history took a significant turn in 1895 when it was ceded to Japan after the First Sino-Japanese War. The subsequent five decades of Japanese colonial rule brought modernization, infrastructure development, and an intertwining of Japanese and Taiwanese cultures. This period's influence is still evident in architecture, education, and cultural practices.

Republic of China and Modernization

After World War II, Taiwan was handed back to the Republic of China (ROC). The ROC government, led by Chiang Kai-shek, established its seat in Taipei, marking the beginning of a new era. As Taiwan embarked on a journey of modernization and economic growth, it preserved its traditional values while embracing innovation, eventually becoming known as one of the "Four Asian Tigers."

A Dynamic Identity

Taiwan's complex history has contributed to a distinctive cultural identity that harmonizes various cultural threads. Traditional practices like ancestor worship and temple festivals continue to thrive alongside technological advancements. Temples adorned with intricate carvings stand as testament to the island's spiritual legacy, while bustling night markets and modern skyscrapers showcase its dynamism.

Festivals and Customs

Taiwan's calendar is punctuated with vibrant festivals that showcase its multicultural heritage. The Lunar New Year, Dragon Boat Festival, and Mid-Autumn Festival are celebrated with fervor, offering visitors a chance to immerse themselves in the traditions, rituals, and joyous spirit of the Taiwanese people.

Language and Cuisine

Mandarin Chinese is the official language, but many people also speak Taiwanese Hokkien and indigenous languages. This linguistic diversity reflects Taiwan's multicultural character. Taiwanese cuisine is equally diverse, blending flavors from China, Japan, and Southeast Asia. From night market snacks to elaborate banquets, food plays a central role in Taiwanese culture.

Preserving the Past, Embracing the Future

Taiwan's historical and cultural landscape is a captivating journey that unveils the island's dynamic evolution. As you explore its ancient temples, modern museums, bustling cities, and tranquil villages, you'll witness the harmonious coexistence of tradition and progress, creating an experience that's both enriching and enlightening.

Embrace the stories of Taiwan's past and present, and you'll discover a destination that's as fascinating as it is welcoming.

- *Weather and Best Time to Visit*

One of the most appealing aspects of traveling to Taiwan is its diverse climate and the range of experiences it offers throughout the year. From sunny beach days to mist-shrouded mountain hikes, Taiwan's weather paints a vibrant backdrop for your journey. To make the most of your visit, understanding the island's seasonal variations is crucial.

Seasonal Overview:

- Spring (March to May): Spring is a wonderful time to visit Taiwan. The weather is mild, with comfortable temperatures and blooming flora painting the landscapes in vibrant colors. Cherry blossoms adorn parks and gardens, creating picture-perfect scenes.

- Summer (June to August): Summer brings warmth and occasional rainfall. This is the peak tourist season due to school holidays. Coastal areas, like Kenting, become popular for beach activities, while mountainous regions offer respite from the heat.

- Autumn (September to November): Many travelers consider autumn the best time to visit Taiwan. The temperatures are pleasant, rainfall decreases, and the landscapes are bathed in a palette of fall colors. It's an ideal time for outdoor adventures and exploring the countryside.

- Winter (December to February): Winter in Taiwan is relatively mild, especially along the coast. In the north, you might experience occasional rain, while the central and southern regions enjoy drier and cooler weather. High mountain areas, such as Alishan and Yangmingshan, experience cold temperatures and even snowfall.

Best Time to Visit:

The "best" time to visit Taiwan largely depends on your preferences and the type of experiences you seek:

- Outdoor Enthusiasts: Spring and autumn are prime seasons for outdoor activities like hiking, cycling, and exploring nature reserves. The weather is comfortably cool, and the landscapes are at their most stunning.

- Beach Lovers: Summer is perfect for those who want to bask in the sun and enjoy water sports. Coastal areas offer a range of beach resorts and water-based activities.

- Cultural Explorers: Throughout the year, Taiwan hosts various cultural festivals and events. However, visiting during Lunar New Year (January or February) provides a unique chance to witness traditional celebrations.

- Budget Travelers: Consider traveling during the shoulder seasons (spring and autumn). You'll find fewer crowds and potentially lower prices on accommodations and flights.

Weather Tips:

- Rainfall: Taiwan's weather can be unpredictable due to its mountainous terrain. Always pack a light rain jacket or umbrella, especially if you're visiting during the rainy season.

- Mountain Areas: If you plan to visit higher elevations like Alishan or Hehuanshan, be prepared for cooler temperatures and varying conditions. Layers are key.

- Typhoon Season: Typhoon season typically runs from June to October. While typhoons are not an everyday occurrence, it's wise to stay informed about weather forecasts during this period.

In conclusion, Taiwan's weather patterns ensure that there's a perfect time for everyone to visit. Whether you're seeking natural beauty, cultural immersion, or a mix of both, understanding the island's climate variations will help you plan a memorable and rewarding journey.

Chapter 2. Essential Travel Information

- *Visa and Entry Requirements*

Traveling to Taiwan offers a doorway into a world of captivating landscapes and rich cultural experiences. To make your journey smooth and hassle-free, it's essential to understand the visa and entry requirements before you embark on your adventure.

Visa Exemption Program

Taiwan's visa policy is designed to accommodate visitors from a wide range of countries, allowing many nationalities to enter without obtaining a visa in advance. Under the Visa Exemption Program, travelers from eligible countries can stay in Taiwan for a specified duration without a visa.

Duration of Stay

The duration of your visa-free stay depends on your nationality and the purpose of your visit. Generally, visitors are granted stays ranging from 14 to 90 days. It's crucial to check the official website of Taiwan's Bureau of Consular Affairs for the most up-to-date information regarding visa exemption and stay duration for your specific country.

Applying for a Visa

If your nationality is not eligible for visa-free entry or if you plan to stay longer than the granted visa-free period, you'll need to apply for a visa before traveling to Taiwan. The type of visa you require will depend on factors such as the purpose of your visit (tourism, business, study, etc.) and the intended duration of stay.

Visitor Visa (Tourist Visa)

The most common type of visa for travelers is the Visitor Visa, which covers tourism, family visits, and short-term business trips. To apply for a Visitor Visa, you'll generally need to provide the following documents:

1. A valid passport with at least six months of validity beyond your intended stay.
2. A completed visa application form.
3. Proof of travel arrangements, such as flight tickets and itinerary.
4. Proof of accommodation during your stay in Taiwan.
5. Sufficient funds to cover your expenses during the visit.

Application Process

Visa applications can typically be submitted to Taiwanese embassies, consulates, or designated visa application centers in your home country. Processing times vary, so it's recommended to apply well in advance of your travel dates.

Visa on Arrival for Some Nationalities

Taiwan also offers a Visa on Arrival (landing visa) program for citizens of certain countries. This allows eligible travelers to obtain a visa upon arrival at designated ports of entry in Taiwan. The Visa on Arrival is often granted for short stays and is intended for tourism purposes.

Extension of Stay

If you're already in Taiwan and wish to extend your stay beyond the granted period, you may be able to apply for an extension through the local National Immigration Agency office. It's important to apply for an extension before your current visa or visa-free stay expires.

Always Verify Requirements

Travel regulations and visa policies can change, so it's crucial to verify the most current requirements before making your travel plans. The official website of the Bureau of Consular Affairs provides comprehensive and updated information on visa and entry requirements for travelers to Taiwan.

Navigating Taiwan's visa and entry requirements ensures that you can focus on immersing yourself in the country's vibrant culture, stunning landscapes, and memorable experiences without any unwanted hiccups.

- *Currency and Banking*

Navigating the financial landscape in Taiwan is a breeze, thanks to a well-developed banking system and a currency that reflects the nation's economic stability. Whether you're planning to explore bustling markets, savor delicious street food, or indulge in shopping sprees, understanding the local currency and banking practices is essential for a seamless travel experience.

Currency: New Taiwan Dollar (TWD)

The official currency of Taiwan is the New Taiwan Dollar, abbreviated as TWD or simply NT$.

Banknotes come in various denominations, including NT$100, NT$500, and NT$1,000, while coins are available in NT$1, NT$5, NT$10, NT$20, and NT$50 denominations. Familiarize yourself with the appearance of the currency and its security features to avoid any confusion or potential counterfeits.

Currency Exchange and ATMs

Currency exchange is readily available at international airports, banks, and authorized exchange offices throughout major cities and tourist areas. It's advisable to compare rates before exchanging currency to ensure you receive the best value for your money. Additionally, automated teller machines (ATMs) are widely available in Taiwan, and major credit and debit cards are accepted at many establishments.

Credit Cards and Payment Methods

Credit cards are commonly accepted at hotels, restaurants, shops, and larger businesses in urban areas. However, it's recommended to carry some cash, especially when exploring local markets, street food stalls, or rural areas where cash transactions are more prevalent. Inform your bank of your travel plans before departing to prevent any issues with using your cards abroad.

Banking Hours

Banks in Taiwan generally operate from Monday to Friday, with some branches also open on Saturdays. Standard banking hours are from around 9:00 AM to 3:30 PM. While some international banks might offer extended hours, it's best to plan your banking needs during the regular hours to avoid any inconvenience.

ATMs and Cash Withdrawals

ATMs are widespread in Taiwan, and many accept international debit and credit cards. Look for ATMs affiliated with major networks like PLUS or Cirrus. Be mindful of potential foreign transaction fees imposed by your home bank. If your card requires a PIN, make sure to have one set before your trip, as some Taiwanese ATMs may require a PIN for transactions.

Currency Tips and Etiquette

- Carry a mix of cash and cards to ensure you're prepared for various payment situations.

- Check with your bank about any partnerships with local banks in Taiwan to reduce withdrawal fees.
- Keep small denominations of cash handy for smaller purchases, such as at street vendors or markets.
- When handling cash, especially at temples or more traditional establishments, use both hands as a sign of respect.

Understanding Taiwan's currency and banking practices will contribute to a smoother and more enjoyable travel experience. By familiarizing yourself with the New Taiwan Dollar and knowing where to find ATMs, exchange services, and places that accept credit cards, you'll be well-equipped to explore the vibrant offerings of this captivating island nation.

- *Language and Communication*

Language is the key to understanding a culture, and in Taiwan, a diverse linguistic landscape reflects the island's rich history and multicultural heritage. While Mandarin Chinese is the official language, the linguistic tapestry of Taiwan also includes various indigenous languages, Hokkien (Taiwanese), Hakka, and even some English due to the island's international connections. Navigating the linguistic landscape of Taiwan adds a layer of depth to your travel experience.

Official Language: Mandarin Chinese

Mandarin Chinese, known as "Putonghua" or "Guoyu" in Taiwan, is the official language and the primary mode of communication for most Taiwanese people. Signs, public transportation announcements, and official documents are typically in Mandarin. While it's possible to get by in many tourist areas with just English, having a few basic Mandarin phrases under your belt can greatly enhance your interactions and show your appreciation for the local culture.

Local Dialects: Hokkien and Hakka

Hokkien, also known as Taiwanese, is spoken widely across the island and is an integral part of daily life, especially among the older generation. It's not uncommon to hear this expressive dialect in markets, local eateries, and street corners. Hakka, another major dialect, is spoken predominantly in certain regions. While Mandarin is understood by most, attempting to use a few phrases in Hokkien or Hakka can be a delightful way to connect with locals and earn smiles of approval.

Indigenous Languages

Taiwan is home to a variety of indigenous peoples, each with their own languages and cultures. While these languages are not widely spoken, efforts are being made to preserve and revitalize them. Some indigenous phrases might appear on street signs or in cultural exhibitions, offering visitors a glimpse into the island's original inhabitants.

English in Taiwan

In urban centers, especially in Taipei, English is spoken and understood by many, especially in businesses and the tourism industry. You'll find signs in English in major cities, public transportation stations, and tourist attractions. Younger Taiwanese are more likely to have a good grasp of English, making communication relatively smooth, particularly in areas frequented by travelers.

Communication Tips

1. Learn Basic Phrases: Familiarize yourself with simple greetings, thank-yous, and basic questions

in Mandarin. Locals appreciate your efforts to engage in their language.

2. Use Gestures: Non-verbal communication, such as pointing, nodding, and smiling, can bridge language barriers effectively.

3. Translation Apps: Download a translation app or keep a pocket phrasebook handy for on-the-go translation assistance.

4. Body Language: Being respectful of local customs, such as bowing slightly when greeting someone older, can go a long way in forging connections.

5. Politeness Matters: Politeness is highly valued in Taiwanese culture. Using honorifics and polite language shows respect and is appreciated.

6. Patience and Openness: Embrace the opportunity to engage with locals and learn about their way of life. Even if conversations are simple, they can lead to memorable experiences.

Embracing the linguistic diversity of Taiwan allows you to connect with its people on a deeper level, offering insights into their history, traditions, and values. As you explore this multifaceted island, language becomes a bridge that connects you to the heart and soul of Taiwan's culture.

Chapter 3. Travel Planning

- *Choosing Your Itinerary*

Designing your itinerary in Taiwan is akin to crafting a masterpiece, where each stroke of exploration reveals a new dimension of this captivating island. Whether you're a solo adventurer, a family seeking bonding experiences, or a couple in search of romantic escapades, Taiwan offers a diverse palette of experiences to suit every traveler's desires. Here's how to curate an unforgettable itinerary that resonates with your unique preferences.

1. Unveiling Urban Wonders

For the urban explorer, Taiwan's cities are an invitation to modernity and cultural immersion. Kick off your journey in Taipei, the vibrant capital, where the iconic Taipei 101 skyscraper pierces the skyline. Dive into the city's bustling night markets, like Shilin and Raohe, where culinary treasures and local crafts abound. Explore historic temples, art galleries, and futuristic districts like Ximending, where fashion and creativity converge.

2. Nature's Embrace

Nature enthusiasts will be enchanted by Taiwan's diverse landscapes. Consider starting your adventure in the Taroko Gorge, a marble wonderland with awe-inspiring cliffs and hiking trails. Journey to Sun Moon Lake for tranquil boat rides and lush scenery, or head south to Kenting National Park for white-sand beaches and coral reefs. Don't miss the breathtaking Alishan National Scenic Area, where misty mountains and ancient forests create an ethereal atmosphere.

3. Cultural Immersion

Immerse yourself in Taiwan's rich cultural tapestry by exploring its historical sites, festivals, and traditions. Visit Tainan, the island's oldest city, where ancient temples and preserved architecture offer a glimpse into Taiwan's past. Time your visit to coincide with festivals like the Lunar New Year or the Lantern Festival for an authentic experience of local celebrations. Engage in traditional tea ceremonies, try your hand at calligraphy, and join a temple procession to connect with Taiwan's heritage.

4. Culinary Exploration

Food lovers will find their paradise in Taiwan, where the street food scene is an attraction in itself. Sample mouthwatering xiao long bao (soup dumplings) in Din Tai Fung, savor beef noodle soup in its birthplace, and indulge in the array of treats at night markets. Consider embarking on a culinary tour to uncover regional specialties like stinky tofu, oyster omelettes, and pineapple cakes.

5. Family-Friendly Adventures

Traveling with family? Taiwan is exceptionally family-friendly, with a myriad of activities that cater to all ages. Taipei's National Palace Museum offers engaging exhibits for kids, while the Taipei Zoo is a hit with animal enthusiasts. Explore the Maokong Gondola and engage in hands-on experiences at the Children's Amusement Park. The island's safety and efficient transportation make family travel a breeze.

6. Romantic Hideaways

Couples seeking romance will find their haven in Taiwan's quieter corners. Stroll through the charming streets of Jiufen, bathed in the warm glow of traditional lanterns. Enjoy a private hot spring retreat in Beitou or indulge in a leisurely bike ride around the picturesque Sun Moon Lake. For a truly enchanting experience, catch the sunset at Cape Eluanbi or take a boat ride along the Lover's River.

No matter your travel style or preferences, Taiwan offers a wealth of experiences that cater to every adventurer's heart. Combine these elements to craft an itinerary that reflects your passions, whether it's exploring urban wonders, immersing yourself in nature, delving into culture, savoring cuisine, creating family memories, or celebrating romance. The beauty of Taiwan lies in its ability to transform every journey into a personalized masterpiece.

- Transportation Options

- Getting in

Getting to Taiwan: Connecting Worlds

Taiwan's allure as a captivating travel destination is matched only by its accessibility. Whether you're journeying from neighboring Asian countries or far-flung corners of the globe, a variety of transportation options await to whisk you away to this island gem.

Air Travel: The Gateway to Taiwan

For international travelers, air travel is the primary and most convenient mode of reaching Taiwan. The Taoyuan International Airport, located in Taipei, serves as the main gateway to the country. This modern airport is well-equipped to handle the influx of visitors and offers a seamless entry experience. From here, you can connect to major cities across the globe, making Taiwan a well-connected hub for global explorers.

Direct Flights from Key Destinations

Taiwan enjoys direct flight connections to major cities in Asia, Europe, North America, and beyond. International airlines offer a range of flight options that cater to various travel preferences and budgets. Flights originating from key cities like Tokyo, Seoul, Hong Kong, Los Angeles, London, and beyond ensure that no matter where you're coming from, reaching Taiwan is a convenient endeavor.

Connecting Flights and Layovers

If you're traveling from destinations that don't have direct flights to Taiwan, connecting flights through nearby international hubs are readily available. Major Asian cities like Hong Kong, Singapore, and Tokyo serve as popular layover points, allowing you to seamlessly bridge the gap between continents and cultures.

Visa Information and Entry Requirements

Before embarking on your journey, it's essential to familiarize yourself with Taiwan's visa policies and entry requirements. Citizens of certain countries may be eligible for visa-exempt entry or visa-on-arrival, allowing for smoother transit through immigration. Always ensure you have the necessary documentation to enter the country, and consider checking the latest travel advisories for any updates.

Ground Transportation upon Arrival

Once you've touched down in Taiwan, a well-connected transportation network awaits to take you to your desired destination. The Taoyuan Airport MRT offers a direct and efficient connection from the airport to Taipei's city center. High-speed rail services, known as the THSR, seamlessly link major cities across the island, making intercity travel a breeze.

Conclusion: Your Journey Begins

The journey to Taiwan is not merely a means of transportation; it's the gateway to a world of captivating landscapes, vibrant cultures, and unforgettable experiences. Whether you're drawn by the bustling streets of Taipei, the serene beauty of the countryside, or the rich historical sites, your adventure starts the moment you board that flight or hop on that connecting train. Get ready to be captivated by Taiwan's magic from the moment you arrive.

- *Getting Around*

Navigating the enchanting landscapes and vibrant cities of Taiwan is a breeze, thanks to its efficient and diverse transportation network. Whether you're exploring the bustling streets of Taipei, traversing the picturesque coastal roads, or venturing into the heart of the island's natural wonders, Taiwan offers a range of transportation options to suit every traveler's preferences and needs.

1. High-Speed Rail (HSR):
Experience the epitome of modern travel on Taiwan's high-speed rail system. Connecting major cities, including Taipei, Taichung, Tainan, and Kaohsiung, the HSR provides an exceptionally fast and comfortable mode of transportation. The trains

are punctual, clean, and equipped with all the amenities you need for a smooth journey.

2. TRA Trains:
Taiwan Railways Administration (TRA) offers an extensive network of regular trains that crisscross the island. Ideal for scenic journeys, these trains offer a more leisurely pace, allowing you to soak in the picturesque landscapes of rolling hills, coastal cliffs, and charming villages.

3. Taipei Metro (MRT):
Taipei's modern and efficient metro system is a traveler's delight. It's the perfect way to explore the city's various neighborhoods, from the historic district of Wanhua to the fashionable streets of Xinyi. The MRT is color-coded, making it easy to navigate, and it's an excellent way to avoid traffic congestion.

4. Buses and Intercity Coaches:
Buses and intercity coaches offer an extensive network that connects cities, towns, and even remote areas. They are a cost-effective way to travel, and the coaches are often equipped with comfortable seats and air conditioning. Local buses are also available within cities for shorter distances.

5. Renting a Scooter or Motorcycle:
For a sense of freedom and exploration, consider renting a scooter or motorcycle. This is a popular choice, especially for navigating smaller towns and rural areas. Just ensure you have the necessary permits and follow local traffic rules.

6. Taxis and Ride-Sharing:
Taxis are readily available in cities and can be hailed on the street or through ride-hailing apps. Ride-sharing apps like Uber and local equivalents offer convenient options for travelers looking for door-to-door service.

7. Domestic Flights:
If you're short on time or want to explore Taiwan's more distant corners, domestic flights are available between major cities. Taiwan's airports are modern and well-connected, offering a quick way to cover long distances.

8. Cycling:
For the eco-conscious traveler and cycling enthusiast, Taiwan has developed an extensive network of cycling paths and routes, especially along its scenic coastlines. You can rent bicycles in many cities and explore at your own pace.

9. Ferries and Boats:
Taiwan's many islands and coastal towns make
ferries and boats an interesting option. Explore the
outlying islands, such as Penghu and Kinmen, or
take a leisurely boat ride along the scenic eastern
coast.

10. Accessibility:
Taiwan's transportation system is designed to be
accessible to people with mobility challenges. Many
stations and vehicles are equipped with ramps and
elevators, and announcements are often made in
multiple languages.

Whether you're a solo traveler, a family with kids,
or a couple seeking romantic escapes, Taiwan's
transportation options cater to all kinds of
adventurers. Remember to plan your routes, check
schedules, and make use of travel cards or passes
for convenience. With such a diverse array of
choices, getting around Taiwan is an integral part of
your journey, offering you the opportunity to
experience the country's beauty and charm from
every angle.

Chapter 4. Solo Traveler's Guide

- *Safety Tips and Concerns*

Exploring Taiwan as a solo traveler can be an incredibly rewarding experience, filled with cultural immersion and personal growth. With its reputation for safety and friendly locals, Taiwan is generally considered a welcoming destination for solo adventurers. However, it's essential to stay vigilant and informed to ensure a smooth and secure journey. Here are some safety tips and concerns to keep in mind:

1. Low Crime Rates:
Taiwan boasts one of the lowest crime rates in the world, making it a relatively safe destination for solo travelers. Violent crime is rare, and the locals are known for their honesty and willingness to help. Nevertheless, it's always wise to take basic precautions, especially in crowded areas or tourist hotspots.

2. Transportation Safety:
Taiwan's public transportation system, including buses and the MRT (Mass Rapid Transit), is efficient and secure. Keep an eye on your belongings while on public transport, and avoid displaying expensive items. Licensed taxis are

generally safe, but always opt for official ones and ask for the meter to be used.

3. Health Precautions:
Taiwan's healthcare system is of high quality, and medical facilities are readily available. It's advisable to have comprehensive travel insurance that covers medical expenses, as well as repatriation in case of emergencies. Stay hydrated, use sunscreen, and take precautions against mosquito-borne illnesses in certain rural areas.

4. Language Barrier:
While many locals, especially in urban areas, have a basic understanding of English, it's helpful to carry a translation app or a pocket phrasebook to communicate effectively, especially in rural or less touristy regions.

5. Cultural Sensitivity:
Taiwanese culture is built on respect and politeness. Familiarize yourself with local customs and etiquette to avoid unintentionally causing offense. Being polite, showing gratitude, and removing your shoes before entering someone's home or certain establishments are important gestures.

6. Scams and Touts:

Scams are relatively uncommon, but it's still advisable to exercise caution. Be wary of overly friendly strangers who may approach you with unsolicited offers. If you encounter any unsolicited assistance or situations that make you uncomfortable, politely decline and move on.

7. Food and Water Safety:
Taiwan's street food is a highlight of any trip, but ensure you choose vendors with proper hygiene practices. Drink bottled or boiled water and be cautious with raw seafood. If you have dietary restrictions or allergies, consider learning key phrases to communicate your needs effectively.

8. Nature and Outdoor Activities:
If you're planning outdoor adventures, such as hiking in Taiwan's stunning national parks, inform someone about your plans and estimated return time. Carry a basic first aid kit, appropriate clothing, and follow marked trails to avoid getting lost.

9. Emergency Contacts:
Store important local contacts in your phone, including the local police (110) and emergency medical services (119). If you're traveling with a

SIM card, ensure you have access to mobile data for navigation and communication.

10. Trust Your Instincts:
Above all, trust your instincts. If a situation doesn't feel right, remove yourself from it. Your safety and well-being are paramount, so don't hesitate to seek help if needed.

By staying informed and practicing common-sense safety measures, your solo journey through Taiwan can be a memorable and enriching adventure. Embrace the culture, connect with locals, and savor every moment of your exploration in this captivating destination.

- Accommodation for Solo Travelers

Traveling solo to Taiwan offers a unique opportunity to explore the island at your own pace and immerse yourself in its diverse culture. Choosing the right accommodation is an essential part of crafting a memorable solo adventure. Fortunately, Taiwan offers a wide range of options to suit every preference and budget, ensuring that your stay is both comfortable and enriching.

1. Hostels: Connecting with Fellow Travelers

Hostels in Taiwan are not just places to rest your head; they are vibrant hubs where like-minded solo travelers gather. They provide a fantastic opportunity to meet new people, share stories, and even find travel companions for day trips. Look for hostels in popular areas like Taipei's Ximending or Tainan's Anping District for a youthful and communal atmosphere.

- Ximen Wow Hostel (Taipei): Situated in the heart of the trendy Ximending neighborhood, this hostel offers stylish dorms, social spaces, and a great location for exploring Taipei's cultural and culinary scene.

- Kenting 157 Boutique Hotel (Kenting): A beachside hostel in the southern town of Kenting, known for its vibrant nightlife and beautiful beaches, offering a laid-back atmosphere and a chance to connect with fellow beach enthusiasts.

2. Guesthouses: A Homely Experience

For solo travelers seeking a more intimate and homely atmosphere, guesthouses are an excellent choice. These accommodations are often run by locals who are eager to share insider tips and recommendations, making your solo journey feel more personal.

- Taitung Story House (Taitung): A charming guesthouse in the scenic city of Taitung, offering cozy rooms, a communal kitchen, and a warm environment that's perfect for unwinding after a day of exploration.

3. Boutique Hotels: Comfort and Style

Boutique hotels offer solo travelers a blend of comfort and style, often with unique designs that reflect Taiwan's artistic culture. These hotels cater to individual needs and provide a luxurious setting to retreat to after a day of adventure.

- The Tango Hotel Taipei Nanshi (Taipei): A stylish boutique hotel in the heart of Taipei's historic district, providing a sophisticated ambiance and easy access to cultural sites and night markets.

4. Capsule Hotels: Compact and Efficient

Capsule hotels are a testament to Taiwan's innovation in hospitality. Ideal for solo travelers seeking privacy and efficiency, these compact accommodations provide a comfortable place to sleep without sacrificing convenience.

- Space Inn (Multiple Locations): With branches across Taipei, Space Inn offers modern capsule accommodations with a futuristic vibe, making it a great choice for solo travelers seeking a unique experience.

Whichever type of accommodation you choose, solo travelers in Taiwan can rest assured that they'll find a welcoming and hospitable environment. From socializing in hostels to enjoying a cozy guesthouse stay or indulging in the comforts of boutique hotels, the accommodation options in Taiwan cater to solo adventurers seeking memorable experiences and meaningful connections.

- Meeting Locals and Making Friends

For solo travelers, Taiwan offers a unique opportunity to connect with locals and make lifelong friendships. Renowned for their warmth, hospitality, and genuine curiosity about the world, Taiwanese people welcome visitors with open arms, creating an environment that is conducive to forming meaningful connections. Here's how you can immerse yourself in the local culture, engage with residents, and forge unforgettable friendships during your solo adventure in Taiwan.

1. Embrace the Night Market Culture

Taiwan's vibrant night markets are not only a treasure trove of tantalizing street food and unique finds but also a prime spot for mingling with locals. Strike up conversations with stall owners, fellow shoppers, and curious onlookers as you sample culinary delights and navigate through bustling aisles. Don't be surprised if you're offered recommendations for the best bites or insider tips on exploring the city.

2. Join Cultural Workshops and Classes

Participating in local workshops and classes offers a fantastic way to connect with both locals and fellow travelers who share similar interests. Enroll in a tea-making class, try your hand at calligraphy, or learn traditional dance moves. These immersive experiences provide a shared learning environment where friendships can naturally blossom.

3. Attend Festivals and Events

Taiwan's calendar is filled with colorful festivals and events that provide an ideal setting to interact with locals. Whether it's the exuberant Lantern Festival, the vibrant Dragon Boat Festival, or the traditional Ghost Month activities, these gatherings offer a chance to engage with locals as they celebrate their heritage and customs.

4. Engage in Outdoor Activities

Joining outdoor activities such as hiking groups, cycling tours, or beach cleanups can introduce you to like-minded individuals who share a passion for exploration and environmental conservation. These shared experiences foster camaraderie and often lead to memorable encounters and friendships.

5. Visit Local Cafes and Tea Houses

Taiwan is famous for its tea culture, and its cozy cafes and traditional tea houses provide a tranquil setting for meaningful conversations. Strike up a chat with the barista or the tea house owner, or simply sit back and enjoy the serene ambiance while observing the daily life around you.

6. Explore Cultural and Historical Sites

As you explore Taiwan's temples, historical sites, and museums, you'll likely encounter friendly locals who are more than willing to share stories about their heritage. Engage in respectful conversations, ask questions, and express genuine interest in learning about the significance of these places.

7. Utilize Language Learning Apps

While many Taiwanese locals have a good command of English, making an effort to learn a few basic Mandarin phrases can go a long way in breaking the ice and showing your genuine interest in their culture. Language learning apps can help you build confidence and create connections.

8. Be Open and Approachable

Approachability is key when it comes to forming connections with locals. Smile, make eye contact, and show genuine curiosity about the people you meet. Be open to spontaneous interactions, whether it's joining a table at a food court or striking up a conversation while waiting for public transportation.

Solo travelers in Taiwan have the privilege of experiencing the warmth of Taiwanese hospitality firsthand. By embracing local customs, attending events, and engaging in conversations, you'll not only enrich your travel experience but also create memories and friendships that will last a lifetime. As you venture through Taiwan, remember that the island's true treasures are the people you meet along the way.

Chapter 5. Top Solo Travel Destinations

- *Taipei*

Taipei, the vibrant heart of Taiwan, welcomes solo travelers with open arms, offering a tapestry of experiences that cater to your adventurous spirit and thirst for discovery. This bustling metropolis seamlessly blends modernity with tradition, creating an urban landscape that's as fascinating as it is inviting. Whether you're seeking cultural immersion, culinary delights, or offbeat explorations, Taipei promises an unforgettable journey for those traveling alone.

Embrace the Urban Pulse

As a solo traveler, Taipei's energy will invigorate your senses. The city's efficient and user-friendly public transportation system, including its extensive metro network, makes navigating a breeze. Begin your adventure by wandering through iconic neighborhoods like Ximending, the youthful and creative heart of the city, where you'll find fashion, street art, and a bustling atmosphere.

Delight in Culinary Adventures

Taipei is a paradise for food enthusiasts, and as a solo traveler, you have the freedom to indulge in a gastronomic journey that suits your preferences. Dive into the sensory explosion of night markets, where stalls line the streets offering delectable treats like bubble tea, oyster omelets, and scallion pancakes. Shilin Night Market is a must-visit, where you can sample the city's most famous street food.

Cultural Encounters

Immerse yourself in Taipei's rich cultural scene by visiting its myriad of temples, museums, and historic sites. Discover the tranquility of Longshan Temple, an important spiritual center, or marvel at the grandeur of the National Palace Museum, home to a stunning collection of Chinese art and artifacts. For a blend of tradition and modernity, explore the historic Dihua Street, lined with traditional shops amidst a contemporary city backdrop.

Panoramic Views and Urban Retreats

For a panoramic view of the city, ascend Taipei 101, once the tallest building in the world. The observatory provides a breathtaking vista that captures Taipei's sprawling landscape, while its unique design is a marvel in itself. Seek moments of respite in Taipei's lush green spaces, such as Daan Forest Park, where you can unwind amidst nature and perhaps strike up conversations with fellow travelers.

Cultural Exchange and Connection

Taipei's friendly locals are renowned for their warmth and hospitality. Engage in cultural exchanges by joining a tai chi session in a park or participating in a traditional tea ceremony. The city's thriving expat and local meetup groups provide opportunities to connect with like-minded individuals, fostering new friendships and shared experiences.

Safety and Convenience

Taipei is consistently ranked as one of the safest cities in the world, making it an ideal destination for solo travelers. English is widely spoken, and signs are often bilingual, offering ease of communication and navigation. The city's robust public transportation system ensures that you can explore confidently, no matter where your curiosity takes you.

Taipei's dynamic blend of modernity and tradition, along with its vibrant cultural scene and culinary delights, makes it an excellent destination for solo travelers. Embrace the freedom to curate your own adventure, whether that entails savoring mouthwatering street food, discovering hidden artistic corners, or forging connections with fellow explorers. Taipei invites you to immerse yourself in its tapestry of experiences, leaving you with memories that will last a lifetime.

- *Jiufen*

Nestled in the lush mountains of northern Taiwan, Jiufen stands as a beacon of charm and nostalgia. This small, historic town is a captivating destination for solo travelers seeking a blend of culture, tranquility, and breathtaking vistas. With its winding streets, traditional architecture, and panoramic views of the Pacific Ocean, Jiufen offers a unique and enriching experience that is perfect for those exploring Taiwan on their own.

Time Travel Through History

Jiufen's history dates back to the Qing Dynasty, and its streets are lined with preserved buildings that harken back to its mining town origins. As a solo traveler, you'll relish the opportunity to meander through these narrow alleys, discovering hidden tea houses, vibrant street markets, and charming boutiques. The town's rich history comes alive through its architecture and winding pathways, allowing you to immerse yourself in the past while creating your own personal journey.

Inspiring Ocean Vistas

One of Jiufen's most enchanting features is its stunning views of the Pacific Ocean. The iconic A-Mei Tea House, perched high on a hill, provides an excellent vantage point to marvel at the azure waters meeting the horizon. As a solo traveler, you can find solace and contemplation in these breathtaking panoramas, capturing moments that resonate deeply within you.

Chasing Culinary Adventures

Jiufen's vibrant food scene is a treasure trove for solo travelers looking to savor Taiwanese delicacies. The town is famous for its traditional street snacks, such as taro and sweet potato balls, as well as its aromatic teas and local specialties. Wandering through Jiufen's market stalls and family-run eateries offers not only a culinary adventure but also a chance to connect with locals and fellow travelers over shared meals.

Engaging Cultural Experiences

For solo travelers seeking cultural immersion, Jiufen delivers in abundance. The town's teahouses are not only places to relax and sip tea; they're also windows into Taiwanese culture and art. Engage in a tea ceremony, learn about the intricate art of calligraphy, or attend a lantern-making workshop to create a lasting memento of your journey.

Tips for Solo Exploration

- Embrace the Freedom: Jiufen's narrow streets and hidden corners are meant to be explored at your own pace. Embrace the freedom to wander without a set agenda, allowing the town's ambiance to guide you.

- Early Mornings and Late Afternoons: To fully appreciate Jiufen's tranquil charm, consider exploring during the early morning or late afternoon when the crowds are thinner and the light is especially magical.

- Local Connections: Strike up conversations with locals and fellow travelers. Jiufen's welcoming atmosphere often leads to meaningful interactions that enhance your solo journey.

- Safety and Respect: While Jiufen is generally safe, remember to take standard precautions as you would in any destination. Respect local customs and etiquette, particularly in temples and cultural sites.

Jiufen, with its captivating history, stunning vistas, delicious cuisine, and engaging cultural experiences, is an ideal destination for solo travelers exploring Taiwan. Whether you're seeking solitude for self-reflection or hoping to forge new connections with locals and fellow explorers, Jiufen welcomes you with open arms and promises an unforgettable journey of discovery.

- Taroko Gorge

If you're a solo traveler seeking awe-inspiring natural beauty, a touch of adventure, and a deep connection with Taiwan's stunning landscapes, then Taroko Gorge is a destination that should be at the top of your must-visit list. Nestled within Taroko National Park, this remarkable gorge offers an unparalleled journey into the heart of Taiwan's rugged and breathtaking terrain. Prepare to be enchanted by its sheer cliffs, rushing rivers, and serene trails that beckon the adventurous soul.

The Solo Adventure Begins

Taroko Gorge welcomes solo travelers with open arms, offering a myriad of experiences that cater to your independent spirit. As you journey through this natural wonderland, you'll find a harmonious blend of tranquility and excitement that will ignite your senses and rejuvenate your spirit.

Highlights for Solo Explorers

1. Eternal Spring Shrine: Begin your exploration with a visit to this iconic shrine nestled into the mountainside. Not only is it a spiritual sanctuary, but it also offers panoramic views of the gorge and its surrounding landscapes.

2. Swallow Grotto Trail: Embark on a solo trek along this trail, which winds through narrow paths carved into the rock walls. Witness the mesmerizing sight of swallows darting around the cliffs while you're surrounded by the gorge's awe-inspiring beauty.

3. Shakadang Trail: Immerse yourself in the lush scenery along this riverside trail. Solo travelers will appreciate the tranquility as they walk alongside the clear turquoise waters of the Shakadang River, surrounded by verdant vegetation.

4. Baiyang Waterfall Trail: For a more adventurous experience, embark on this trail that leads to the stunning Baiyang Waterfall. Walk through tunnels, cross suspension bridges, and enjoy the thrill of getting up close to the cascading waters.

5. Qingshui Cliffs: A short drive from the main gorge area, these dramatic cliffs overlooking the Pacific Ocean are a sight to behold. Solo travelers can marvel at the sheer drop from designated viewpoints or capture the views in solitude.

Solo Traveler Tips

- Safety First: While Taroko Gorge's trails are generally well-maintained, it's important to prioritize your safety. Inform someone about your hiking plans and take necessary precautions, especially if you're embarking on longer treks.

- Early Starts: To fully enjoy the tranquility of the gorge and avoid crowds, start your adventures early in the morning. The magical sunrise illuminating the towering cliffs is a sight you won't want to miss.

- Pack Essentials: Ensure you're well-prepared with essentials like water, snacks, comfortable hiking shoes, a hat, and sunscreen. The climate can vary, so dressing in layers is a good idea.

- Cultural Respect: Remember that Taroko Gorge is not only a natural wonder but also a place of cultural significance for the indigenous people of Taiwan. Show respect for the environment and any signs of spirituality you encounter.

Solo Reflections

As you navigate the trails of Taroko Gorge, the sense of solitude and connection with nature can be deeply enriching. The grandeur of the gorge, coupled with the meditative serenity it offers, makes it a perfect canvas for solo travelers to paint their own adventure. It's a chance to discover not only the physical beauty of Taiwan but also the beauty within yourself as you conquer challenges, embrace solitude, and create memories that will stay with you long after you've left this remarkable landscape behind.

- *Tainan*

For the solo traveler seeking a unique and immersive experience in Taiwan, Tainan beckons with its rich history, cultural tapestry, and serene ambiance. As the oldest city on the island, Tainan boasts a blend of traditional charm and modern vibrancy, making it an ideal destination for those embarking on a journey of self-discovery. From ancient temples and bustling markets to serene gardens and mouth watering street food, Tainan promises an unforgettable solo adventure.

Exploring Tainan's Historical Marvels

Begin your solo journey in Tainan by stepping back in time. The city is adorned with historic temples that hold stories of devotion and perseverance. Marvel at the intricate architecture of the Koxinga Shrine, dedicated to the famed Ming Dynasty military leader, and venture to the Chihkan Tower, where Dutch, Chinese, and Japanese influences are interwoven.

Cultural Immersion and Culinary Delights

Tainan's vibrant culture is best experienced through its lively night markets. Wander through the stalls of the Garden Night Market, where fragrant aromas and colorful displays beckon you to savor local delicacies like oyster omelets, coffin bread, and shrimp rolls. Engage with friendly vendors, practice your bargaining skills, and dive into the heart of Taiwanese street food culture.

An Oasis of Tranquility: Anping District

Escape the bustle and find solace in the Anping District. Roam the tree-lined streets and uncover historical sites like Anping Fort, which stands as a testament to Tainan's maritime history. Don't miss the opportunity to visit Anping Tree House, where a banyan tree has reclaimed an old warehouse, creating an enchanting fusion of nature and architecture.

Reflective Moments at Koxinga Shrine

Find a serene space for reflection at Koxinga Shrine. Nestled amidst lush greenery, this shrine provides a peaceful retreat where you can immerse yourself in meditation or simply appreciate the tranquility of your surroundings. The captivating sea views serve as a reminder of the island's maritime heritage.

Art, Coffee, and Hidden Gems

Tainan's creative spirit is alive in its art districts, such as the Blueprint Cultural and Creative Park. Discover galleries, workshops, and artisanal boutiques, offering a glimpse into the city's contemporary artistic scene. Fuel your explorations with a visit to a quaint café, where you can unwind, sip on aromatic local brews, and connect with fellow travelers.

Local Interactions and Authentic Encounters

The heart of Tainan lies in its people, and solo travelers have the opportunity to form meaningful connections with the locals. Join a guided walking tour to gain insights into the city's history and culture from passionate guides. Engage in conversations with shopkeepers, share a smile with fellow wanderers, and embrace the warmth of Tainan's welcoming community.

Practical Tips for Solo Adventurers

- Navigating the City: Tainan is well-connected by buses and affordable taxis. Consider renting a bicycle to explore the city at your own pace.

- Language: While English may not be widely spoken, locals are usually eager to help. Having a translation app can be handy.

- Accommodation: Choose from a range of hostels, guesthouses, and boutique hotels that cater to solo travelers, providing opportunities to meet fellow adventurers.

- Safety: Tainan is generally safe for solo travelers, but exercise usual caution and avoid dimly lit areas at night.

Embrace the Soul of Tainan

Tainan offers solo travelers a remarkable blend of history, culture, and tranquility that invites introspection and connection. As you navigate the city's labyrinthine streets, savor its flavors, and soak in its stories, you'll discover that Tainan is not just a destination; it's an experience that lingers in the heart long after your solo adventure comes to an end.

Chapter 6. Family-Friendly Travel

- *Child-Friendly Accommodation*

Traveling with children is an enriching experience, and finding the right accommodation can make all the difference in ensuring a comfortable and enjoyable trip for the whole family. Taiwan offers a variety of child-friendly accommodation options that cater to the needs of parents and kids alike. From spacious rooms to entertaining facilities, these accommodations understand the unique requirements of traveling families.

Family-Oriented Hotels with Playful Amenities

Many hotels across Taiwan specialize in catering to families, offering a range of amenities to keep kids entertained and parents relaxed. These family-oriented hotels often feature dedicated play areas, children's pools, and even supervised activities, allowing parents to enjoy some downtime while their little ones are engaged in safe and enjoyable activities.

Suggested Accommodations:
1. Howard Plaza Hotel Taipei: This centrally located hotel in Taipei offers spacious family suites equipped with child-friendly amenities. The hotel's

kids' club provides a range of supervised activities, while the outdoor pool and children's pool promise endless water fun.

2. Fleur de Chine Hotel, Sun Moon Lake: Situated by the stunning Sun Moon Lake, this luxury resort offers family suites with lake views. The hotel's Kids' Club organizes arts and crafts activities, allowing children to unleash their creativity while parents explore the surroundings.

Resorts with Adventure and Nature Activities

Taiwan's diverse landscapes provide ample opportunities for outdoor adventures, and some resorts have embraced this by offering family-friendly activities like guided nature walks, biking tours, and even farm experiences. These accommodations allow families to bond while exploring Taiwan's beautiful countryside.

Suggested Accommodations:
1. Leofoo Resort Guanshi: Located near Leofoo Village Theme Park, this resort is a dream for kids. With safari-themed rooms and a variety of family activities, including a water park and wildlife encounters, it's a perfect choice for a fun-filled family getaway.

2. Lalu, Sun Moon Lake: This luxurious resort offers family packages that include lake-view rooms, family activities, and even opportunities for stargazing. The resort's location provides easy access to Sun Moon Lake's natural beauty.

Apartment Rentals with Home-Like Comfort

For families seeking a more home-like environment, apartment rentals can be an excellent choice. These accommodations provide spacious living areas, kitchens, and often multiple bedrooms, giving families the flexibility to cook their own meals and maintain routines.

Suggested Accommodations:
1. Airbnb: Airbnb offers a wide range of family-friendly apartment rentals in various parts of Taiwan. From Taipei to Kaohsiung, you can find comfortable and well-equipped apartments suitable for families of all sizes.

2. Booking.com: This platform also lists a variety of apartment rentals with family-friendly amenities. Look for options with high guest ratings and positive reviews from families who have stayed there.

When booking child-friendly accommodation in Taiwan, consider your family's preferences, the location's proximity to attractions, and the amenities provided. Whether you choose a playful hotel with on-site activities or a cozy apartment rental, Taiwan's hospitality will ensure that your family enjoys an unforgettable and hassle-free vacation.

- *Safety Considerations*

When embarking on a family adventure in Taiwan, safety is undoubtedly a top priority. Thankfully, Taiwan is known for its overall safety, efficient public services, and family-friendly environment. However, like any travel destination, there are a few important safety considerations to keep in mind to ensure a worry-free and enjoyable trip for you and your loved ones.

1. Health and Medical Services:
   - Taiwan's healthcare system is excellent, with modern medical facilities and well-trained professionals. Keep a list of emergency numbers, local hospitals, and clinics handy.
   - It's advisable to have travel insurance that covers medical emergencies, especially if you or your family members have specific medical needs.

2. Food and Water Safety:
   - Generally, Taiwan's food hygiene standards are high. Stick to busy eateries and popular night markets to ensure the freshness of the food.
   - Drink bottled water or use a water purifier to avoid consuming tap water. Bottled water is widely available.

3. Child-Friendly Facilities:
   - Most major cities and tourist areas in Taiwan are equipped with family-friendly amenities, including changing stations, nursing rooms, and child-friendly restaurants.
   - Shopping malls and entertainment centers often have designated play areas for children.

4. Traffic Safety:
   - Taiwan's public transportation, including buses and trains, is well-maintained and safe. However, be cautious when crossing streets, as traffic can be fast-paced in some areas.
   - If you're traveling with young children, use appropriate car seats or booster seats when using taxis or renting a car.

5. Personal Belongings:

- Taiwan is generally safe from petty crime, but it's wise to keep an eye on your belongings, especially in crowded places such as markets and transportation hubs.
- Consider using money belts or pouches to keep your important documents and valuables secure.

6. Natural Disasters:
- Taiwan is prone to typhoons and earthquakes, particularly during certain seasons. Stay updated on weather forecasts and follow any advisories from local authorities.
- Hotels and accommodations are well-prepared for these situations, so familiarize yourself with evacuation procedures if necessary.

7. Cultural Sensitivity:
- Taiwanese culture places great emphasis on respect and courtesy. Teach your children about local customs, such as removing shoes when entering homes or certain establishments.
- Encourage your family to be respectful when visiting temples and religious sites.

8. Emergency Contacts:
- Keep a list of emergency contacts, including the local police, medical services, and your country's embassy or consulate.

9. Language Barrier:
  - While many people in Taiwan speak English, especially in urban areas, having a translation app or a few basic phrases in Mandarin can be helpful.

10. Plan and Communicate:
  - Plan your activities with the needs and preferences of your family members in mind. Communicate your plans to ensure everyone is on the same page and feels comfortable.

Traveling with your family in Taiwan can be an enriching experience, and by following these safety considerations, you'll be better equipped to enjoy every moment of your journey. Remember that preparation and awareness are key to a successful and enjoyable family adventure in this vibrant and welcoming country.

- *Kid-Friendly Activities*

Traveling with kids in Taiwan is an absolute delight, as the island offers a wide array of family-friendly activities that cater to the interests of both young adventurers and their parents. From interactive museums to vibrant amusement parks, Taiwan ensures that every member of the family has an unforgettable experience. Here are some of the top kid-friendly activities that will make your family vacation in Taiwan truly special:

1. National Museum of Natural Science (Taichung)
   - Explore a captivating world of science, dinosaurs, and space exploration.
   - Interactive exhibits, including the exciting earthquake simulator.
   - Children's Discovery Room offering hands-on learning experiences.

2. Taipei Children's Amusement Park (Taipei)
   - A sprawling park with numerous rides, including roller coasters and carousels.
   - Themed areas such as Space Land and Discovery Land for diverse adventures.
   - Seasonal events and parades to keep the whole family entertained.

3. Leofoo Village Theme Park (Hsinchu County)
   - A thrilling theme park featuring Safari, Wild West, and Arabian Nights zones.
   - Animal encounters with elephants, lions, and other fascinating creatures.
   - Exciting rides and performances for kids of all ages.

4. Taipei Zoo (Taipei)

- Home to a wide variety of animals from around the world.
- Giant panda exhibit is a major highlight, drawing visitors of all ages.
- Educational exhibits and opportunities for animal encounters.

5. Maokong Gondola (Taipei)
- Enjoy a scenic cable car ride up to Maokong, known for its tea plantations.
- Panoramic views of Taipei city and surrounding nature.
- Family-friendly tea houses and easy hiking trails.

6. Yehliu Geopark (New Taipei City)
- Witness the fascinating rock formations, including the iconic "Queen's Head."
- Geological wonders that spark children's curiosity.
- A blend of education and natural beauty in a captivating outdoor setting.

7. Formosan Aboriginal Culture Village (Nantou)
- A cultural theme park showcasing Taiwan's indigenous heritage.
- Traditional performances, tribal villages, and authentic crafts.

- Amusement park rides and lush landscapes for a perfect family day out.

8. Taoyuan Land Art Festival (Taoyuan)
   - An annual event featuring large-scale outdoor art installations.
   - Interactive art pieces that encourage play and exploration.
   - Creative and engaging experiences for both kids and adults.

9. Taipei Children's Recreation Center (Taipei)
   - Indoor play space with various activities for different age groups.
   - Arts and crafts, interactive games, and imaginative play areas.
   - A wonderful escape on rainy days or for a fun break from sightseeing.

10. National Palace Museum (Taipei)
    - Engage kids in history through ancient artifacts and treasures.
    - Family-friendly guided tours and activity stations.
    - Unique learning opportunities within a cultural context.

In Taiwan, the options for kid-friendly adventures are as diverse as the island's landscapes. From exciting theme parks to educational museums and interactive experiences, your family will create cherished memories together while discovering the magic of Taiwan.

Chapter 7. Kid-Focused Destinations

- Taipei Children's Amusement Park

Nestled amidst the vibrant tapestry of Taipei's urban landscape, the Taipei Children's Amusement Park stands as a testament to the city's dedication to wholesome family entertainment. This enchanting haven of fun and laughter has been delighting visitors, both young and young at heart, for decades.

A Wonderland of Playful Adventures

Step into a world where imagination takes flight, and every corner is a gateway to boundless joy. The Taipei Children's Amusement Park is a sprawling wonderland filled with an array of rides, games, and attractions designed to spark the delight of its little visitors. From exhilarating roller coasters that send hearts racing to gentle carousels that twirl amidst melodies, the park offers a diverse range of experiences suitable for children of all ages.

Highlight Attractions

- Flying Elephant Ride: Watch the world transform into a mosaic of colors as you soar gently above the park, offering a bird's-eye view of the surroundings.

- Merry-Go-Round: A classic favorite, the merry-go-round invites children to hop onto beautifully adorned horses and whirl to the tune of whimsical melodies.

- Children's Theater: Immerse yourselves in captivating storytelling and performances designed to captivate young minds.

- Outdoor Water Play Area: On warm days, the outdoor water play area becomes a sanctuary of refreshing fun, where splashes and laughter go hand in hand.

- Ferris Wheel: Ascend to breathtaking heights on the Ferris wheel, granting panoramic vistas of Taipei's skyline, creating unforgettable memories.

Thoughtfully Crafted for Families

The Taipei Children's Amusement Park is more than just an amusement destination; it's a place where families come together to create lasting memories. With its emphasis on safety, cleanliness, and family-friendly facilities, parents can relax knowing that their children are in good hands.

Educational and Interactive Zones

Beyond the exhilarating rides, the park also features educational zones that engage curious minds. The Children's Science Museum offers hands-on exhibits that inspire learning through play, fostering a sense of wonder about the world around us. These interactive experiences make the park an ideal destination for families seeking both entertainment and education.

Culinary Delights and Picnic Spots

Treat your taste buds to an array of delectable snacks and treats available throughout the park. From cotton candy clouds to savory bites, the culinary offerings ensure that every moment spent at the park is a feast for the senses. For those looking to enjoy a leisurely picnic, the park provides well-maintained green spaces perfect for relaxation and bonding.

Practical Information

- Location: 55, Sec. 5, Chengde Road, Shilin District, Taipei City, Taiwan
- Opening Hours: Vary by season, typically 9:00 AM to 5:00 PM

- Admission: Affordable entry fees; various pricing options for rides and attractions
- Accessibility: Well-connected by public transportation; parking available

The Taipei Children's Amusement Park encapsulates the essence of family togetherness and the exuberance of childhood. As you explore Taipei with your little adventurers, make sure to carve out time for a visit to this enchanting park, where laughter reverberates in the air, and every moment is a treasure trove of joy.

- *National Museum of Natural Science*

Nestled in the heart of Taichung, the National Museum of Natural Science stands as a captivating testament to Taiwan's rich natural heritage and scientific curiosity. This sprawling complex is not just a museum; it's a journey through time, space, and the wonders of the natural world. From captivating exhibitions to interactive displays, the museum offers an educational and awe-inspiring experience for visitors of all ages.

The National Museum of Natural Science is a treasure trove of knowledge, offering a comprehensive exploration of Earth's history, evolution, and biodiversity. As you step inside, you're immediately transported to a world of discovery through its carefully curated exhibits, interactive installations, and engaging presentations.

Exhibition Highlights

1. Space Pavilion: Delve into the mysteries of the universe, from celestial bodies to the intricacies of space exploration. The planetarium within the pavilion offers immersive shows that unravel the secrets of the cosmos.

2. Botanical Garden: Wander through lush gardens that showcase Taiwan's diverse flora. From the towering banyan trees to intricate orchids, this outdoor sanctuary provides a serene escape within the city.

3. Life Science Hall: Embark on a journey through the evolution of life, from prehistoric creatures to modern-day wildlife. The life-like dioramas and interactive displays bring the natural world up close and personal.

4. Human Cultures Hall: Learn about the rich tapestry of human history and culture, from ancient civilizations to the indigenous tribes of Taiwan.

Artifacts, multimedia presentations, and recreations offer a glimpse into the past.

What sets the National Museum of Natural Science apart is its commitment to interactive learning. The museum's hands-on exhibits engage visitors in a dynamic learning experience, making complex scientific concepts accessible to all. From simulating earthquakes to exploring the depths of the ocean, visitors can actively participate in scientific experiments and discoveries.

Families with children will find the museum particularly engaging, as it offers educational and entertaining activities that spark curiosity and imagination. The Kid's Discovery Hall is a haven for young explorers, with interactive displays and games designed to teach them about the natural world while having fun.

Practical Information

- Location: No. 1, Guanqian Road, North District, Taichung City, Taiwan.
- Opening Hours: The museum is usually open from 9:00 AM to 5:00 PM, Tuesday to Sunday.

- Admission: The entry fee varies for different parts of the museum. Combination tickets for multiple areas are available.
- Guided Tours: Guided tours and educational programs are offered; check the museum's website for details.
- Accessibility: The museum is wheelchair accessible, with ramps and elevators.

A visit to the National Museum of Natural Science is a journey of discovery, enlightenment, and appreciation for the natural world. Whether you're a nature enthusiast, a science buff, or a family looking for an educational day out, this museum offers an unforgettable experience that will leave you with a newfound understanding of our planet's past, present, and future.

- Leofoo Village Theme Park

Nestled at the foothills of the breathtaking Baoshan Mountain range, Leofoo Village Theme Park stands as a captivating testament to the allure of imagination and thrills. This expansive amusement park, situated just a stone's throw away from Taipei, beckons visitors of all ages to step into a world where excitement and fantasy intertwine seamlessly.

A Whimsical Wonderland of Attractions

Leofoo Village Theme Park is a realm of boundless entertainment, offering an impressive array of attractions designed to cater to a wide range of tastes and preferences. Divided into three distinct sections – Arabian Kingdom, Wild West, and South Pacific – the park exudes an atmosphere reminiscent of three different worlds, each with its own unique charm and character.

Arabian Kingdom: A Tale of Enchantment

Step into the Arabian Kingdom, where the exotic allure of the Middle East comes to life. Lavish palaces, intricate mosaics, and bustling marketplaces set the scene for a magical adventure. Thrill-seekers can brave heart-pounding roller coasters like "Sultan's Adventure" and "Flying Carpet," while families can enjoy whimsical rides and interactive attractions suitable for all ages.

Wild West: Yee-Haw Adventures Await

For those with a penchant for the Wild West, this section of the park will transport you to a time of cowboys and outlaws. Wooden facades and dusty streets create an authentic atmosphere as visitors enjoy attractions like the exhilarating "Mine Train" coaster and the interactive shooting game "Wild West Shootout."

South Pacific: Tropical Escapes

The South Pacific section offers a tropical paradise filled with lush foliage, vibrant colors, and Polynesian vibes. Relaxing rides like the "Waikiki Wave" and "Waikiki Jungle Carousel" provide a delightful escape for families, while the "Ring of Fire" and "Waikiki Odyssey" cater to those seeking an adrenaline rush.

Safari Adventures: A Thrilling Safari Experience

One of the most remarkable features of Leofoo Village Theme Park is its Safari area. Home to a diverse range of animals, including majestic lions, agile cheetahs, and towering giraffes, this safari experience brings the magic of Africa right to Taiwan. The "African Safari" ride allows visitors to get up close to these magnificent creatures in a simulated African savannah environment.

Entertainment and Beyond

Beyond the rides, Leofoo Village Theme Park offers an array of live performances, parades, and shows that add to the overall enchantment. Witness spectacular stunt shows, vibrant parades featuring larger-than-life characters, and captivating performances that showcase the cultural diversity of the themed sections.

Practical Information

- Location: Hsinchu County, approximately 1.5 hours from Taipei.
- Opening Hours: The park's operating hours vary, so it's recommended to check the official website for up-to-date information.
- Tickets: Ticket options include one-day passes and combination passes for multiple parks.
- Accessibility: The park is designed to be family-friendly, with rides suitable for all ages.

Leofoo Village Theme Park invites you to embark on a journey that transcends reality and embraces the extraordinary. Whether you're a thrill-seeker, a family with children, or simply someone looking to bask in the magic of a whimsical universe, Leofoo Village Theme Park promises an unforgettable experience that will linger in your memories long after you leave. Step into a world where adventure and fantasy unite, and let the enchantment of Leofoo Village be your gateway to joy, wonder, and pure exhilaration.

- Kenting National Park (Family Beach Activities)

Nestled along Taiwan's southernmost coastline, Kenting National Park is a paradise of sun, sand, and surf that beckons families to create lasting memories in its picturesque embrace. This tropical haven offers a plethora of family-friendly beach activities, making it an ideal destination for parents and children seeking adventure, relaxation, and quality time together.

1. Beach Picnics and Sandcastle Building

The sandy shores of Kenting's beaches are the perfect canvas for family bonding. Spread out a colorful picnic blanket and indulge in a delightful spread of local treats while the kids build sandcastles that rival sand sculptures. The gentle waves and serene atmosphere provide a backdrop for a day of simple pleasures.

2. Snorkeling and Underwater Exploration

Dive into a world of vibrant marine life by engaging in family-friendly snorkeling adventures. The crystal-clear waters around Kenting are home to coral reefs teeming with colorful fish, making it an excellent opportunity for kids and adults alike to witness the wonders beneath the waves. Snorkeling tours with knowledgeable guides are available for a safe and educational experience.

3. Banana Boat Rides and Water Sports

For families seeking a bit more excitement, Kenting's beaches offer an array of water sports that cater to various comfort levels. Hop on a thrilling banana boat ride as a group, take a leisurely paddle on a kayak, or try your hand at windsurfing. These exhilarating activities guarantee laughter-filled hours of aquatic enjoyment.

4. Sunset Strolls and Family Photoshoots

As the sun begins its descent, the beaches of Kenting transform into a captivating scene of golden hues and pastel skies. Take a leisurely sunset stroll with your loved ones, collecting seashells and capturing the enchanting backdrop in family photos that will be cherished for years to come.

5. Beach Campfires and Nighttime Magic

Create magical moments by the sea as the day turns into night. Many beaches in Kenting permit campfires, allowing families to gather around crackling flames, share stories, and toast marshmallows under the starry sky. It's a chance to connect with nature and one another in a unique setting.

6. Exploring Nature and Wildlife

Beyond the beaches, Kenting National Park offers a plethora of family-friendly trails and nature walks. Embark on a guided hike through lush forests, where kids can learn about the park's diverse flora and fauna. Keep an eye out for the playful Formosan macaques and vibrant bird species that call this area home.

7. Dolphin and Whale Watching Tours

Kenting's proximity to the ocean means families can embark on exciting dolphin and whale watching tours. Witness these majestic creatures in their natural habitat, as they breach and swim gracefully through the waves. It's a rare and awe-inspiring experience that both kids and adults will cherish.

Whether you're building sandcastles, exploring underwater worlds, or simply enjoying the sun-drenched shores, Kenting National Park offers a treasure trove of family beach activities that cater to all ages. The memories you create here, amidst the beauty of nature and the joy of shared experiences, are certain to be woven into the fabric of your family's story.

Chapter 8. Romantic Escapes

- *Couples-Friendly Accommodation*

When it comes to a romantic getaway, Taiwan offers a plethora of accommodation options that promise not only comfort and luxury but also an enchanting backdrop for couples to create lasting memories. Whether you're celebrating an anniversary, honeymoon, or simply seeking a romantic escape, Taiwan's hospitality industry is ready to indulge your senses.

1. Luxury Retreats

Taiwan boasts an array of luxurious hotels and resorts that cater to couples looking for a lavish escape. From Taipei's urban oases with stunning city views to secluded hillside retreats in the heart of nature, these properties combine impeccable service with opulent amenities. Consider properties like:

   - The Regent Taipei: Overlooking the vibrant cityscape, this renowned hotel pampers couples with spacious suites, spa treatments, and fine dining experiences.

- Silks Place Taroko: Nestled at the entrance of Taroko Gorge, this resort offers rooms with private balconies showcasing the breathtaking gorge views, creating an intimate and serene atmosphere.

2. Boutique Charm

For couples who value uniqueness and charm, Taiwan's boutique hotels offer an intimate and personalized experience. These accommodations often feature creative design, locally inspired decor, and an ambiance that lends itself to romance. Notable options include:

- Folks Hotel: Situated in the heart of Tainan's historic district, this boutique hotel's nostalgic design and elegant atmosphere provide a cozy haven for couples.

- The Humble House Taipei: With its minimalist elegance and artistic touches, this hotel's rooms and rooftop bar provide a chic setting for couples to unwind.

3. Secluded Resorts

Couples seeking seclusion and tranquility will find Taiwan's countryside dotted with charming bed-and-breakfasts and boutique lodges. These hidden gems offer a perfect escape from the hustle and bustle of city life. Consider:

- Les Champs: Located in the Alishan area, this bed-and-breakfast is surrounded by tea plantations and offers cozy rooms and serene natural surroundings.

- The Lalu Sun Moon Lake: Set against the picturesque Sun Moon Lake, this resort blends seamlessly with its environment, providing an idyllic haven for couples.

4. Hot Spring Retreats

Taiwan is famous for its natural hot springs, and couples can indulge in the ultimate relaxation by staying in hot spring resorts. Unwind together in private open-air baths while enjoying breathtaking views. Don't miss:

- Spring City Resort: Offering hot spring villas with stunning vistas, this resort in Beitou, Taipei, lets couples rejuvenate in mineral-rich waters.

- Guanwu Villa: Nestled in the mountains, this resort allows couples to soak in secluded hot spring pools surrounded by lush greenery.

5. Romantic Glamping

For a unique twist on romantic accommodation, consider the rising trend of glamping (glamorous camping). Enjoy the outdoors without sacrificing comfort at:

- Gloria Manor: This elegant glamping resort in Kenting offers luxurious tents equipped with modern amenities, providing a blend of nature and comfort.

- Star Haus: Located in the rural beauty of Nantou, this glamping spot offers stargazing opportunities and cozy lodgings, perfect for couples seeking a celestial experience.

From luxurious urban getaways to serene countryside escapes, Taiwan's diverse range of couples-friendly accommodation ensures that every couple's dream of a romantic retreat becomes a reality. Each stay offers a unique blend of comfort, luxury, and ambiance, enhancing the magic of your journey through this enchanting island.

- Romantic Dining and Experiences

For couples seeking to infuse their journey with romance, Taiwan offers a plethora of enchanting experiences that cater to every kind of love story. From intimate candlelit dinners with panoramic views to strolls through lantern-lit streets, this island destination creates an unforgettable backdrop for love to flourish. Here are some of the most romantic dining and experiences that Taiwan has to offer:

1. Sunset at Lover's Bridge, Tamsui

Immerse yourselves in the warm hues of a Tamsui sunset as you stroll hand in hand along Lover's Bridge. This iconic spot is particularly captivating during the golden hour, when the sky becomes a canvas of orange and pink hues. As the sun dips below the horizon, the views of the coastline and city lights create an idyllic setting for a romantic evening.

2. Dining in the Sky at Taipei 101

Elevate your romantic experience at Din Tai Fung, located within the iconic Taipei 101 skyscraper. Reserve a window table to enjoy panoramic views of the city's twinkling lights while indulging in delectable dumplings and gourmet Taiwanese cuisine. The combination of fine dining and breathtaking vistas sets the stage for a truly memorable night.

3. Maokong Gondola Ride and Tea Houses

Embark on a gondola ride up to Maokong, a tea-growing area overlooking Taipei. Surrounded by verdant hills, you'll find charming tea houses where you can savor aromatic blends while gazing at the city below. The tranquil ambiance and lush scenery create an intimate escape for couples looking to unwind and connect.

4. Release Sky Lanterns in Pingxi

Visit the picturesque village of Pingxi, known for its traditional sky lantern festival. You and your partner can inscribe your wishes and dreams on a lantern before releasing it into the night sky. As your lantern joins the twinkling constellations, it's a poignant moment of unity and shared aspirations.

5. Moonlit Beach Walk in Kenting

The beaches of Kenting exude a different kind of charm under the moonlight. Take a leisurely stroll along the shoreline, hand in hand, as the waves softly kiss the sand. The tranquility and intimacy of the moment make for a perfect romantic escapade.

6. Hot Springs Retreat in Beitou

Beitou, a district of Taipei, is renowned for its natural hot springs. Book a private hot spring bath for two and unwind in mineral-rich waters surrounded by lush greenery. The serene atmosphere and healing properties of the springs provide a soothing backdrop for couples to relax and rejuvenate.

7. Historic Stroll in Jiufen

Wander through the lantern-lit streets of Jiufen, a historic town known for its charming architecture and narrow alleyways. The nostalgic ambiance, coupled with the glimmering lights, creates an enchanting setting for a leisurely evening walk, punctuated by stops at traditional teahouses and food stalls.

Whether it's celebrating a special occasion, rekindling romance, or simply cherishing each other's company, Taiwan's romantic dining and experiences are designed to create lasting memories. From breathtaking vistas to intimate moments in quaint locales, this diverse and captivating island provides the ideal canvas for love to flourish.

- *Relaxing Spas and Hot Springs*

Amidst Taiwan's bustling cities and breathtaking landscapes lies a sanctuary of relaxation and rejuvenation – its world-renowned spas and hot springs. The island's rich geothermal activity has blessed it with a plethora of natural thermal springs, making it a haven for those seeking to unwind in soothing mineral-rich waters. Whether you're a weary traveler, a couple seeking romance, or a family in need of rejuvenation, Taiwan's spas and hot springs promise a therapeutic escape like no other.

Taipei's Urban Oasis

Even in the heart of Taiwan's capital city, tranquility can be found. Taipei boasts an array of luxurious spas and wellness centers that offer an oasis of calm amidst the city's energy. Step into a realm of sensory indulgence, where expert therapists pamper you with ancient techniques and modern treatments. From traditional Chinese massages to aromatherapy sessions, these urban sanctuaries provide an ideal respite for travelers looking to unwind after a day of exploration.

Beitou's Natural Bounty

Just a short ride away from Taipei lies Beitou, a district famous for its natural hot springs. Beitou's hot spring resorts blend seamlessly into the lush surroundings, offering a unique experience where relaxation meets nature. Here, you can soak in private mineral baths, public hot spring pools, and even foot spas along the banks of the Beitou River. The tranquil Japanese-style Thermal Valley, known as "Hell Valley," showcases the area's geothermal wonders and provides an insight into the region's volcanic activity.

Yangmingshan National Park's Hidden Gems

Yangmingshan National Park, another gem near Taipei, is home to various hot spring options that cater to different preferences. Plunge into a private outdoor bath while admiring panoramic mountain views, or immerse yourself in public hot spring pools surrounded by vibrant vegetation. The park's unique mix of hot springs, volcanic landscapes, and refreshing hiking trails makes it an ideal destination for nature lovers and relaxation seekers alike.

Jiaosi's Serene Escape

Venture east to Jiaoxi in Yilan County, a region celebrated for its natural beauty and therapeutic waters. Here, hot spring resorts offer a serene escape nestled between rolling hills and verdant fields. Dip into the mineral-rich springs, believed to have various health benefits, and let your worries melt away in the embrace of nature.

Alishan's Mountain Retreats

In the highlands of Alishan, where misty mountains and ancient forests reign, you'll find hot spring retreats that provide a different kind of relaxation. Imagine unwinding in outdoor baths as you breathe in the crisp mountain air and listen to the soothing sounds of nature. These elevated hot springs offer a tranquil escape, especially after a day of exploring Alishan's breathtaking landscapes.

Practical Tips:

- Reservations: Many hot spring resorts require reservations, especially during peak seasons. It's wise to book in advance to secure your spot.

- Etiquette: Follow local hot spring etiquette, which often includes showering before entering the baths and wearing appropriate swimwear.

- Health Benefits: The mineral-rich waters are said to offer various health benefits, from improved circulation to skin rejuvenation.

- Time of Day: Consider visiting hot springs at different times of day to experience the changing ambiance – from morning freshness to evening serenity.

Indulging in Taiwan's hot springs and spa retreats is not just about physical relaxation; it's an immersion into a centuries-old tradition of wellness and rejuvenation. Whether you seek respite from the city, a break from adventure, or simply a chance to soak in natural beauty, Taiwan's hot springs promise an experience that will soothe your body, mind, and soul, leaving you refreshed and renewed for the rest of your journey.

Chapter 9. Enchanting Couple Destinations

- *Sun Moon Lake*

Nestled in the heart of Taiwan's lush central mountains, Sun Moon Lake is a jewel-like destination that exudes romance and tranquility, making it the perfect retreat for couples seeking a magical escape. This picturesque lake, surrounded by mist-covered peaks and emerald forests, offers an enchanting setting where you and your partner can create unforgettable memories.

Scenic Splendor

As you arrive at Sun Moon Lake, you'll be captivated by the breathtaking beauty that unfolds before you. The lake itself is shaped like a crescent moon on one side and a round sun on the other, lending it its poetic name. Azure waters glisten under the sunlight, reflecting the verdant landscape and sky above. The surrounding hills, adorned with tea plantations and hiking trails, complete the ethereal panorama.

Romantic Activities

1. Boat Cruises: Set the mood with a leisurely boat cruise on Sun Moon Lake. Glide across the serene

waters, hand in hand, as you take in the spectacular views and cool mountain breeze. Sunset and moonlit cruises are particularly romantic, casting the lake in a warm, golden glow.

2. Cycling Exploration: Rent a tandem bike and embark on a romantic cycling journey along the lake's shores. The well-maintained paths lead you through charming villages, lakeside parks, and hidden coves. Stop for a lakeside picnic or simply relish in the joy of exploring together.

3. Wenwu Temple: Visit the elegant Wenwu Temple, dedicated to Confucius and Guan Gong, where the scent of incense and the tranquil ambiance create a peaceful atmosphere. The temple's hillside location offers panoramic views of the lake and its surroundings.

4. Xuanzang Temple: Perched on the tranquil hills surrounding the lake, Xuanzang Temple provides a quiet sanctuary for couples seeking moments of reflection and togetherness. The serene surroundings and distant views of the lake create an ideal setting for romantic contemplation.

5. Cable Car Adventure: Take a cable car ride to the Formosan Aboriginal Cultural Village, where you

can explore the indigenous culture of Taiwan. The journey up offers stunning aerial views of the lake, while the theme park itself provides interactive experiences for couples.

Intimate Dining Experiences

Sun Moon Lake offers a delightful array of dining options that cater to couples seeking intimate moments:

1. Lakeside Dining: Indulge in a candlelit dinner at one of the lakeside restaurants. As the sun sets behind the mountains, enjoy a delectable meal featuring local ingredients and flavors.

2. Floating Restaurants: Experience a unique dining adventure on a floating restaurant. These traditional wooden boats have been transformed into intimate dining venues, offering exquisite dishes while you gently float on the lake.

3. Teahouses: The lake's surrounding areas are known for their tea plantations. Visit a teahouse nestled amidst tea fields, where you and your partner can savor the art of tea preparation while soaking in the serene ambiance.

Sun Moon Lake weaves an enchanting tapestry of romance, natural beauty, and cultural charm that beckons couples to create cherished memories together. Whether you're enjoying a leisurely boat ride, exploring lakeside temples, or sharing a quiet moment over a cup of tea, Sun Moon Lake offers an idyllic escape where love blossoms amidst Taiwan's breathtaking landscapes.

- Alishan National Scenic Area

Nestled amidst the central mountain range of Taiwan, the Alishan National Scenic Area presents an ethereal landscape that evokes romance and wonder. For couples seeking a getaway that blends breathtaking natural beauty with moments of tranquility and intimacy, Alishan is the perfect destination to create cherished memories together.

Enchanting Sun Rises Above the Clouds

One of the most enchanting experiences in Alishan is witnessing the sunrise from the famous Alishan Sunrise Platform. Wake up early, hand in hand, and ascend through mist-laden forests to the platform. As the first light of day breaks, you'll be treated to a mesmerizing spectacle as the sun paints the sky with hues of pink, gold, and orange, while the rolling sea of clouds below you shimmers in the dawn's embrace. This magical moment is bound to strengthen the bond between you and your partner.

Intimate Strolls Amidst Ancient Trees

Alishan is renowned for its ancient cypress trees, some of which are over a thousand years old. Hand in hand, explore the forested trails that wind through these majestic groves. The aptly named "Lover's Trail" offers a particularly romantic route, inviting you to immerse yourselves in the peaceful ambiance of the woods and admire the towering trees, whose branches seem to reach out and embrace the sky.

A Journey Through Time: The Alishan Forest Railway

Embark on a nostalgic train journey aboard the Alishan Forest Railway, a heritage line that winds its way through verdant landscapes and mountain vistas. The small, old-fashioned train cars add a touch of vintage charm to your journey, evoking a sense of timeless romance. The rhythmic chugging of the train and the ever-changing panoramas make this ride an intimate and unforgettable experience for couples.

Starlit Nights and Celestial Dreams

As night falls over Alishan, the sky transforms into a canopy of twinkling stars. The high altitude and clear air create perfect conditions for stargazing. Find a quiet spot away from the lights, lay a blanket down, and cuddle up under the starlit sky. The celestial beauty above serves as a backdrop for intimate conversations and shared dreams, reminding you of the vast universe that surrounds your love story.

Romantic Accommodations and Dining

Alishan offers a range of cozy accommodations nestled within the mountains, from charming lodges to boutique inns. Imagine waking up to the sounds of nature and enjoying a hearty breakfast overlooking breathtaking vistas. Many of these accommodations provide private balconies or terraces, allowing you to savor the natural beauty in seclusion. Don't miss the opportunity to relish a romantic dinner with local Taiwanese cuisine, perfectly complementing the romantic atmosphere.

For couples seeking a romantic retreat that seamlessly blends natural beauty, tranquility, and shared experiences, Alishan National Scenic Area is a haven that promises to ignite the flames of love and create lasting memories. Whether it's a sunrise embraced by clouds, a stroll through ancient forests, or a starlit night, Alishan provides the canvas on which your romantic journey can unfold.

- *Penghu Islands*

Nestled in the cerulean embrace of the Taiwan Strait lies a hidden gem that whispers of romance and serenity – the Penghu Islands. This enchanting archipelago, composed of 90 islets and islands, is a haven for couples seeking to escape the ordinary and immerse themselves in a world of breathtaking landscapes, intimate moments, and timeless experiences.

Unveiling the Beauty of Penghu

As you set foot on the sun-kissed shores of Penghu, you'll be greeted by a pristine coastline that stretches as far as the eye can see. Azure waters gently lap against powdery white sands, creating a canvas of tranquility that invites you to explore its hidden coves, secret beaches, and secluded spots. Whether you're strolling hand in hand along the shoreline or enjoying a private picnic on a deserted beach, Penghu's coastal beauty sets the stage for unforgettable moments with your loved one.

Sunsets and Starlit Skies

Prepare for an immersive symphony of colors as the sun dips below the horizon, painting the sky with hues of orange, pink, and gold. The sunsets in Penghu are legendary, casting an ethereal glow over the sea and transforming the island's landscapes into dreamlike vistas. For the ultimate romantic experience, consider embarking on a sunset cruise, where you can sip champagne, share laughter, and watch as the sun's last rays dance on the water.

As the sun bids its adieu, the stage is set for another mesmerizing spectacle – Penghu's starlit skies. Away from the city lights, the islands offer an unobstructed view of the celestial wonders above. Imagine lying hand in hand under a blanket of stars, lost in each other's company as constellations reveal their stories overhead.

Intimate Dining Experiences

Penghu's romantic essence extends to its culinary offerings. Set the tone for an unforgettable evening by indulging in a candlelit dinner by the sea. From fresh seafood caught that day to delectable local specialties, Penghu's restaurants offer not just a feast for the palate, but a feast for the senses. Imagine savoring a sumptuous meal as the moon's reflection dances on the water, creating an ambiance that words can't capture – it's an experience that's all about you and your partner.

Island Adventures for Two

For couples seeking adventure, Penghu has a plethora of activities that promise excitement and bonding. Rent a scooter and explore the islands at your own pace, discovering hidden coves, charming villages, and breathtaking viewpoints. Snorkeling and diving in Penghu's crystal-clear waters reveal a world of vibrant marine life and colorful coral reefs, creating unforgettable underwater memories together.

Cherished Moments, Lasting Memories

Penghu Islands offer an idyllic setting for couples to create memories that will be etched in their hearts forever. Whether you're celebrating a special occasion, rekindling your love, or simply escaping to a romantic paradise, Penghu's allure lies in its ability to slow down time and create moments that are exclusively yours.

From tranquil beaches and fiery sunsets to starry nights and intimate dining, Penghu Islands present an invitation to weave your love story into the fabric of its natural wonders. Let the islands' enchanting embrace draw you closer as you celebrate your love amidst this captivating tapestry of beauty, peace, and shared experiences.

- Rainbow Village

Nestled in the heart of Taiwan, the charming Rainbow Village stands as a testament to the transformative power of art and love. This vibrant village, located on the outskirts of Taichung, is not only a visual marvel but also an enchanting destination for couples seeking a unique and romantic experience.

A Riot of Colors and Creativity

Rainbow Village, once a military housing complex, was saved from demolition by the colorful brush strokes of a single resident, Huang Yung-Fu, also known as "Grandpa Rainbow." With boundless creativity and a heart full of love for his home, Grandpa Rainbow began painting the walls, floors, and even ceilings of the village with an explosion of bright hues and intricate designs. Today, his whimsical artwork covers every inch of the village, transforming it into a living, breathing masterpiece.

Stroll Through a Fairytale World

For couples visiting Taiwan, Rainbow Village offers an enchanting escape into a world that feels straight out of a storybook. Hand-in-hand, you can wander through narrow lanes adorned with colorful characters, playful animals, and vibrant landscapes. As you explore, you'll find charming murals that tell stories of the village's history and showcase Grandpa Rainbow's heartwarming journey.

A Captivating Backdrop for Love

Rainbow Village is not just a feast for the eyes; it's also a perfect backdrop for couples looking to capture romantic moments together. The kaleidoscope of colors creates a dreamy and whimsical atmosphere, providing countless photo opportunities. Whether it's stealing a kiss by a painted mural or simply holding hands against the vibrant backdrop, Rainbow Village offers a unique setting for your love story.

Interactive Art and Heartfelt Messages

As you stroll through the village, you'll find interactive artworks that invite you to be a part of the creative experience. Grab a paintbrush and add your own touches to designated spots, leaving a piece of your love story behind. You can also discover hidden nooks adorned with heartfelt messages and wishes from visitors all around the world, creating a sense of connection and unity.

Memories to Cherish

A visit to Rainbow Village is more than just a sightseeing excursion – it's an immersive experience that allows couples to connect with each other and with the vibrant spirit of creativity. Whether you're capturing snapshots together, leaving your mark on the village's walls, or simply taking in the sheer joy of Grandpa Rainbow's art, the memories you make here will be cherished for a lifetime.

Practical Tips for Couples

- Timing: Visit Rainbow Village during the daytime to fully appreciate the vibrant colors and details of the artwork.

- Photography: Don't forget your camera or smartphone! The vivid colors make for stunning photos.

- Interactive Fun: Participate in the interactive painting areas – it's a unique way to create memories together.

- Local Souvenirs: Support the village by purchasing souvenirs like postcards, keychains, and artwork created by Grandpa Rainbow.

- Romantic Stroll: Take your time as you stroll through the village. It's not just about the visuals; it's about savoring the experience with your loved one.

Rainbow Village is more than just a tourist attraction; it's a celebration of art, love, and the indomitable human spirit. For couples seeking a place that reflects the kaleidoscope of emotions in their relationship, this whimsical haven in Taiwan is the perfect canvas to paint memories that will remain vivid forever.

Chapter 10. Taiwanese Culture and Traditions

- *Etiquette and Customs*

Traveling to Taiwan offers not only a chance to explore breathtaking landscapes and savor mouthwatering cuisine but also an opportunity to engage with a rich tapestry of customs and etiquette that reflect the island's unique cultural identity. As a visitor, showing respect for local customs will enhance your experience and help you connect more deeply with the people and their way of life.

1. Respect for Elders and Hierarchy
Taiwanese society places great importance on respecting elders and acknowledging social hierarchy. It's customary to address older individuals with titles like "Auntie" or "Uncle" even if they're not family. Additionally, when handing or receiving objects, use both hands as a sign of respect, especially when interacting with elders.

2. Greetings and Politeness
Greet people with a slight nod or a friendly smile. A handshake is also acceptable, especially in more formal settings. Remember that Taiwanese people are generally reserved, so avoid loud conversations or boisterous behavior in public places. Maintain a

polite and composed demeanor, and you'll find locals responding warmly.

3. Gift-Giving Etiquette

Gift-giving is a common practice in Taiwan, and it's appreciated as a gesture of goodwill. When presenting a gift, use both hands, and expect the recipient to express modesty by initially refusing the gift. It's considered polite to insist a couple of times before they finally accept it. Gifts should be wrapped neatly, and avoid giving items in sets of four, as the word for "four" sounds like the word for "death" in Mandarin.

4. Dining Etiquette

Taiwanese cuisine is a centerpiece of local culture, and there are specific dining customs to keep in mind. It's courteous to wait for the host to begin eating before you start your meal. When using chopsticks, never stick them upright into a bowl of rice, as this resembles a funeral ritual. Instead, place them horizontally across your bowl. Burping after a meal is considered a compliment to the chef, signifying you've enjoyed the meal.

5. Temple Etiquette

Taiwan is dotted with beautiful temples, each with its own rituals and practices. When visiting a temple, dress modestly and remove your shoes before entering. It's customary to make a small donation and light incense as a sign of respect. Taking photos is usually allowed, but always ask for permission before photographing people, especially during religious ceremonies.

6. Shoes and Footwear
Wearing shoes indoors is generally considered impolite. It's customary to remove your shoes before entering someone's home or certain establishments, such as temples. Many places provide slippers for guests to wear indoors.

7. Public Behavior
Taiwan is known for its cleanliness and orderliness. It's important to dispose of trash properly and follow recycling guidelines. Keep in mind that smoking is prohibited in many public spaces, including restaurants and indoor areas. Always adhere to designated smoking zones.

8. Language and Communication
Learning a few basic phrases in Mandarin Chinese, such as "hello" (nǐ hǎo) and "thank you" (xièxiè), goes a long way in showing respect for the local culture. While English is spoken in tourist areas,

making an effort to communicate in the local language is appreciated.

By embracing these etiquette and customs, you'll not only show your respect for Taiwan's traditions but also open doors to genuine interactions and a more immersive travel experience. As you journey through the island's vibrant landscapes and engage with its warm-hearted people, remember that your mindful and respectful behavior will undoubtedly create cherished memories and lasting connections.

- *Festivals and Celebrations*

Taiwan's cultural tapestry is woven with a rich array of festivals and celebrations that reflect its diverse history and heritage. These events provide an unparalleled opportunity to witness the island's traditional customs, religious devotion, and communal spirit. As you journey through Taiwan, make sure to align your visit with some of these captivating festivals to truly immerse yourself in the local culture.

1. Lunar New Year (Spring Festival)

Lunar New Year, also known as Spring Festival, is the most important celebration in Taiwan. Taking place between late January and mid-February, this event marks the beginning of the lunar calendar and is characterized by colorful parades, lion dances, and vibrant firework displays. Families gather for reunion dinners and exchange red envelopes filled with money as symbols of good luck and fortune.

2. Lantern Festival

Held on the 15th day of the Lunar New Year, the Lantern Festival illuminates the night sky with a kaleidoscope of glowing lanterns. From traditional paper lanterns to elaborate light displays, cities and towns across Taiwan come alive with this enchanting spectacle. The release of sky lanterns is a highlight, symbolizing the release of worries and wishes for the upcoming year.

3. Qingming Festival (Tomb-Sweeping Day)

Observed in early April, Qingming Festival is a time for paying respects to ancestors by cleaning their gravesites and making offerings. It's a tradition rooted in reverence for the past and filial piety. During this period, hillsides come alive with vibrant flowers, as families come together for picnics and outdoor activities.

4. Dragon Boat Festival

Celebrated on the fifth day of the fifth month of the lunar calendar (usually June), the Dragon Boat Festival commemorates the life and death of the ancient poet Qu Yuan. Festivities include dragon boat races, where teams paddle to the rhythm of drums, and the consumption of zongzi – sticky rice dumplings wrapped in bamboo leaves.

5. Ghost Month (Hungry Ghost Festival)

August marks the Ghost Month, a time when it is believed that the gates of the afterlife open, allowing spirits to roam the earthly realm. Various rituals, including burning paper offerings and hosting elaborate performances, are held to appease and honor these spirits. Theatrical performances and outdoor films are also common during this month.

6. Mid-Autumn Festival

Taking place on the 15th day of the eighth lunar month (usually September), the Mid-Autumn Festival centers around the full moon and the sharing of mooncakes. Families gather to enjoy moonlit nights, light lanterns, and relish mooncakes – round pastries filled with sweet fillings or salted egg yolks – as they celebrate unity and togetherness.

7. Double Tenth National Day

On October 10th, Taiwan commemorates its National Day with patriotic parades, flag-raising ceremonies, and cultural performances. It marks the anniversary of the Wuchang Uprising, a pivotal event that led to the overthrow of the Qing Dynasty and the founding of the Republic of China.

8. Mazu Pilgrimage

The annual Mazu Pilgrimage is a remarkable display of faith and devotion. Celebrated in various cities, most notably in Tainan and Dajia, this religious procession honors Mazu, the Goddess of the Sea and Protector of Seafarers. The streets come alive with colorful parades, elaborate floats, and traditional performances.

Immerse yourself in the captivating rhythms of Taiwan's festivals and celebrations, where age-old traditions blend harmoniously with the modern world. These cultural events offer a unique window into the heart and soul of Taiwan, creating memories that will stay with you long after your journey has ended.

- *Arts and Crafts*

In the heart of East Asia, Taiwan's artistic heritage is as diverse and intricate as the threads woven into its traditional textiles. Steeped in centuries of cultural exchange and craftsmanship, the island has nurtured a thriving arts and crafts scene that beautifully marries age-old techniques with contemporary creativity. From pottery to calligraphy, weaving to woodworking, exploring Taiwan's arts and crafts is a journey into the soul of its culture.

Preserving Tradition through Handicrafts

Taiwanese craftsmanship is a testament to the island's dedication to preserving its rich heritage. Delve into the world of indigenous artistry, where each tribe boasts distinctive weaving and beadwork styles that reflect their connection to nature and ancestral wisdom. The intricate patterns and vibrant colors tell stories that have been passed down through generations.

Ceramics: The Art of Fire and Earth

Taiwan's ceramics industry stands as a testament to the delicate balance between tradition and innovation. Visit the pottery villages of Yingge and Sansia to witness skilled artisans shaping clay into exquisite teapots, vases, and delicate porcelain pieces. These centers not only honor ancient craftsmanship but also push the boundaries of design, blending traditional aesthetics with contemporary sensibilities.

Lacquerware: A Fusion of Art and Utility

For centuries, Taiwanese artisans have perfected the craft of lacquerware, transforming humble materials into exquisite works of art. Intricately carved lacquerware boxes, plates, and bowls reflect a harmonious union of aesthetics and practicality. These pieces showcase the delicate artistry of lacquer application, often adorned with elaborate motifs and mother-of-pearl inlays.

Textiles: Weaving Stories of Tradition

Taiwan's textiles are a testament to the island's history of trade and cultural exchange. The weaving communities in places like Lukang and Meinong are known for their mastery of techniques, producing stunning silk, cotton, and bamboo textiles. Witness traditional looms in action and marvel at the intricate designs that echo the beauty of Taiwan's landscapes and traditions.

Calligraphy and Painting: Capturing the Essence

Embrace the art of calligraphy and painting, deeply rooted in Taiwan's Confucian heritage. Traditional characters come alive on rice paper as skilled calligraphers use brush and ink to capture the essence of poetry and philosophy. Explore galleries and workshops in Taipei and Kaohsiung to witness the mesmerizing transformation of empty space into profound expressions.

Marketplaces and Craft Fairs: Souvenirs of Authenticity

Immerse yourself in Taiwan's arts and crafts scene by exploring vibrant markets and craft fairs. From the iconic Shilin Night Market in Taipei to the charming weekend markets in Tainan, you'll find an array of handmade treasures, from intricate ceramics and delicate textiles to unique jewelry and contemporary art pieces. These markets offer not just objects, but stories and connections to the artisans behind the creations.

Crafting New Horizons: Contemporary Artistry

Taiwan's creative spirit doesn't just dwell in its traditional crafts. The island's contemporary arts scene is a dynamic blend of innovation and expression, with modern galleries, street art, and multimedia installations. Discover the bustling creative districts of Taipei, like Huashan 1914 Creative Park, where local artists and international talents converge to redefine artistic boundaries.

Participate and Learn: Workshops and Classes

Why not dive into Taiwan's artistic world yourself? Many places offer workshops and classes, allowing you to learn traditional techniques firsthand. Whether it's a pottery class, calligraphy workshop, or weaving experience, these immersive opportunities offer a deeper understanding of Taiwan's artistic heritage.

In Taiwan, arts and crafts are more than just objects; they're an exploration of culture, history, and the creative spirit that binds generations. As you navigate through Taiwan's bustling markets, serene workshops, and vibrant galleries, you'll find yourself woven into the intricate tapestry of

Taiwanese creativity, a testament to the island's enduring passion for beauty and expression.

Chapter 11. Cultural Landmarks

- *Chiang Kai-shek Memorial Hall*

Nestled at the heart of Taipei, the Chiang Kai-shek Memorial Hall stands as a testament to Taiwan's complex history, its resilient spirit, and its commitment to preserving its cultural heritage. This iconic landmark is more than just a monument; it's a place of reverence, reflection, and unity.

A Grand Tribute to a Complex Figure

The Chiang Kai-shek Memorial Hall was erected in honor of Chiang Kai-shek, a towering figure in Taiwan's history. Chiang served as the leader of the Republic of China for decades and played a pivotal role in shaping the nation's trajectory. The hall was completed in 1980, four years after Chiang's passing, as a tribute to his contributions.

Architectural Splendor and Symbolism

The memorial's architecture is a masterpiece that merges traditional Chinese design elements with modern aesthetics. The most prominent feature is the majestic blue-tiled octagonal roof, representing the number eight significance in Chinese culture – a symbol of fortune and prosperity. The color blue pays homage to the blue skies over Taiwan.

Guarding History: The Honor Guard Ceremony

Visitors to the memorial are treated to the spectacle of the Honor Guard Ceremony, a solemn ritual that takes place in front of the main hall. Dressed in immaculate uniforms, honor guards conduct precise drills and choreographed movements in homage to Chiang Kai-shek's legacy and the values he championed.

The Enchanting Memorial Park

The memorial hall is encompassed by a vast and tranquil park that provides a peaceful respite from the city's hustle and bustle. As you stroll through the lush gardens, you'll encounter serene ponds, intricate pavilions, and thought-provoking sculptures that add an artistic dimension to the site.

Preserving Taiwan's Identity

The Chiang Kai-shek Memorial Hall transcends its historical association and serves as a symbol of Taiwan's ongoing journey towards self-identity and unity. It's a place where diverse generations come to learn about their past, understand the challenges that have been overcome, and appreciate the strides taken towards democracy, freedom, and cultural preservation.

Visitor Tips

1. Exploring the Hall: Venture into the memorial's interior to discover exhibitions chronicling Taiwan's history and Chiang Kai-shek's role. The museum offers insights into the nation's political evolution and the challenges it has faced.

2. Changing of the Guard: Plan your visit to coincide with the Honor Guard Ceremony, which takes place on the hour from 9 AM to 4 PM. Witnessing the precision and dedication of the guards is a captivating experience.

3. Serene Reflection: Take a leisurely stroll through the surrounding gardens to find tranquility amidst the city's energy. The lotus ponds, pavilions, and well-maintained landscapes make for a perfect spot to relax and reflect.

4. Photography: Capture the awe-inspiring architecture, especially during the golden hours

when the sunlight bathes the memorial in a warm glow.

The Chiang Kai-shek Memorial Hall serves as a bridge between Taiwan's storied past and its promising future. Its architectural grandeur, historical significance, and serene surroundings make it an essential stop for anyone seeking to understand the essence of Taiwan – a nation that cherishes its heritage while looking steadfastly ahead.

- *Longshan Temple*

Nestled within the vibrant streets of Taipei, Longshan Temple stands as a timeless testament to Taiwan's rich cultural tapestry and spiritual heritage. This iconic temple is not just a religious site; it's a living embodiment of the island's history, resilience, and devotion. A visit to Longshan Temple offers travelers an immersive experience that transcends time, inviting them to witness the convergence of tradition and modern life.

A Glimpse into the Past: History and Significance

Longshan Temple, also known as Lungshan Temple, traces its origins back to the early 18th century, when it was founded by settlers from Fujian province in China. Throughout its history, the temple has undergone several renovations and survived natural disasters, wars, and social transformations. It stands today as a testament to the unwavering faith of the Taiwanese people and their determination to preserve their cultural heritage.

Architectural Beauty and Artistic Splendor

As you step into the temple's intricately carved entrance gate, you're greeted by a world of architectural wonder. The main hall, dedicated to the bodhisattva Guanyin, exudes an air of serenity with its ornate wood carvings, vibrant paintings, and delicate porcelain figurines. The temple's design showcases a fusion of Chinese and Taiwanese architectural styles, creating a unique visual tapestry that captivates the senses.

Spiritual Experience and Rituals

Longshan Temple is a living sanctuary where locals and visitors alike come to offer prayers, seek blessings, and find solace. The temple's inner courtyard features a central lotus pond, where worshippers light incense, make offerings, and engage in traditional rituals that have been practiced for generations. The atmosphere is a harmonious blend of devotion, reverence, and a sense of community.

Ancient Traditions and Cultural Expressions

Throughout the year, Longshan Temple comes alive with a calendar of vibrant festivals and events that showcase Taiwan's rich cultural heritage. Festivals like the Lunar New Year, Qingming Festival, and Mid-Autumn Festival transform the temple into a kaleidoscope of colors, incense smoke, and lively processions. These celebrations offer a unique window into Taiwanese spirituality and provide an opportunity for travelers to participate in the island's age-old traditions.

Guidance for Visitors

When visiting Longshan Temple, it's important to be respectful of the temple's sacred nature and the worshippers present. Here are a few tips to make the most of your experience:

1. Dress Modestly: Wear appropriate clothing that covers your shoulders and knees as a sign of respect.

2. Observe Quietude: Maintain a peaceful demeanor while exploring the temple to honor the worshippers' devotion.

3. Photography Etiquette: Ask for permission before taking photos, especially of worshippers or during ceremonies.

4. Participate Mindfully: If you choose to participate in any rituals, do so with sincerity and respect for the customs.

Visiting Longshan Temple is a Journey Through Time

Longshan Temple is more than just a place of worship; it's a living embodiment of Taiwan's history, culture, and faith. Exploring its halls and witnessing the devotion of its visitors is an opportunity to connect with the soul of Taiwan, where tradition and modernity come together in a profound and beautiful way. Whether you're seeking spiritual enlightenment, cultural insight, or simply a moment of tranquility in the midst of a bustling city, Longshan Temple welcomes you with open arms and a sense of timeless wonder.

- *National Palace Museum*

Nestled in the lush landscapes of Taipei, the National Palace Museum stands as a beacon of Taiwan's rich cultural heritage and artistic legacy. This remarkable institution houses one of the world's most extensive collections of Chinese art and artifacts, offering visitors an enchanting journey through centuries of history, craftsmanship, and artistic expression.

A Glimpse into the Collection

The National Palace Museum's vast collection spans over 8,000 years of Chinese history, with artifacts ranging from the exquisite to the profound. Wander through its expansive halls to discover ancient paintings, intricate calligraphy, delicate porcelain, majestic sculptures, and awe-inspiring jade carvings. Each piece tells a story of emperors, scholars, artisans, and dynasties that have shaped China's cultural landscape.

History and Significance

Originally established in Beijing's Forbidden City during the Qing Dynasty, the museum's collection was relocated to Taiwan in the aftermath of the Chinese Civil War. This move safeguarded the invaluable artifacts from destruction and ensured their preservation for future generations. Today, the National Palace Museum serves as a testament to the commitment of preserving and sharing Chinese culture and history.

Highlights of the Museum

Among the museum's most celebrated treasures is the "Jadeite Cabbage with Insects," a delicate sculpture carved from a single piece of jade. This piece is symbolic of fertility, prosperity, and artistic excellence. Equally captivating is the "Meat-shaped Stone," a masterpiece carved from banded jasper that remarkably resembles a succulent piece of roasted pork.

The museum's paintings showcase the evolution of Chinese art, from traditional landscapes to intricate portraits. The "Admonitions Scroll," a prized possession, is a remarkable example of Chinese ink painting, depicting scenes of ancient court life and moral lessons.

Exhibition Halls and Special Displays

The National Palace Museum's collection is vast, and its exhibitions rotate regularly, ensuring that return visitors are greeted with fresh marvels. Permanent galleries offer a chronological journey through China's dynasties, while temporary exhibitions shed light on specific themes, artists, or periods, providing a dynamic experience for visitors.

Visitor Experience and Tips

To make the most of your visit to the National Palace Museum, consider these tips:

1. Audio Guides: Audio guides are available in multiple languages, providing in-depth information about key artifacts and their historical context.

2. Guided Tours: Joining a guided tour offers insights and stories that might otherwise go unnoticed.

3. Allow Ample Time: The museum's vast collection deserves several hours of exploration, so plan your visit accordingly.

4. Souvenir Shop: The museum's gift shop offers a variety of quality souvenirs, from replica artifacts to traditional crafts.

Preserving the Past, Enriching the Present

A visit to the National Palace Museum is a journey that bridges the gap between the past and the present, allowing you to immerse yourself in the artistic and cultural achievements of ancient China. Whether you're an art aficionado, a history enthusiast, or simply curious about the world's heritage, this museum promises a deeply immersive and enlightening experience that captures the essence of Taiwan's commitment to preserving and sharing its cultural treasures.

- Lukang Historic Area

Nestled on the western coast of Taiwan, the Lukang Historic Area stands as a living testament to the island's rich history and cultural heritage. With its well-preserved architecture, charming streets, and historic sites, Lukang offers travelers a captivating journey through time.

A Glimpse into the Past

Lukang, meaning "Deer Harbor" in Mandarin, was once a bustling trading port during the Qing Dynasty. Today, it retains much of its old-world charm, inviting visitors to wander along its cobbled streets and soak in the ambiance of a bygone era.

The blend of Chinese, Dutch, and Japanese influences is evident in its architecture and landmarks, showcasing the layers of history that have shaped the town.

Historic Architectural Treasures

The streets of Lukang are lined with well-preserved traditional houses, temples, and shrines that transport visitors back in time. One of the most iconic structures is the Lukang Longshan Temple, a masterpiece of Taiwanese temple architecture adorned with intricate wood carvings and ornate decorations. As you stroll through the town, you'll discover stunning examples of courtyard homes, each telling a story of its own.

Mazu Pilgrimage and Festivals

Lukang is particularly renowned for its association with Mazu, the Goddess of the Sea. The annual Mazu Pilgrimage is a captivating spectacle, where devotees carry the deity's statue through the town's narrow streets in a vibrant procession. This religious event is a vibrant tapestry of faith, cultural heritage, and community unity.

Lukang Arts and Crafts

Artisans in Lukang have been honing their crafts for generations. Delve into the world of traditional handicrafts, from intricately woven bamboo products to delicate porcelain figurines. Lukang's artistic heritage is celebrated through workshops and stores that offer visitors the chance to witness these crafts being created and even try their hand at making them.

Local Delicacies and Snacks

Exploring Lukang's historic sites and streets can work up an appetite, and luckily, the town offers a delightful array of local treats. Sample the famed Lukang mochi, a chewy rice cake filled with a variety of sweet or savory fillings. Don't miss the opportunity to savor traditional Taiwanese snacks, such as oyster omelets and meatball soup, at the charming local eateries.

Preserving Heritage for Generations

The Lukang Historic Area has not only preserved its architectural heritage but also its strong community bonds and local traditions. As you interact with the residents, you'll gain insights into the daily life of the town's inhabitants and witness the efforts made to safeguard the area's cultural legacy for generations to come.

Practical Tips for Visiting

- Getting There: Lukang is easily accessible by train, bus, or car from major cities like Taipei and Taichung.

- Best Time to Visit: Spring and fall offer the most pleasant weather for exploration.

- Exploration: Wear comfortable shoes for walking as Lukang is best explored on foot.

- Cultural Etiquette: When visiting temples and historic sites, remember to dress modestly and be respectful of local customs.

A trip to the Lukang Historic Area is like stepping into a time capsule that showcases Taiwan's cultural tapestry and historical significance. Its cobblestone streets, ornate temples, and artisanal crafts provide a remarkable opportunity to immerse yourself in the beauty of a town that echoes with centuries of stories and traditions.

Chapter 12. Nature and Adventure

- *Hiking and Trekking*

Taiwan's rugged terrain, diverse landscapes, and extensive network of trails make it a haven for hikers and trekkers of all levels. Whether you're a seasoned mountaineer or a casual walker, the island's trails offer an unforgettable journey through dense forests, towering peaks, cascading waterfalls, and breathtaking vistas. Lace up your boots, grab your backpack, and get ready to explore some of the most spectacular hiking destinations in Asia.

Trails for Every Adventurer

From leisurely strolls to challenging ascents, Taiwan's hiking trails cater to a wide range of preferences. Novices can revel in the tranquility of trails like the Pingxi Crags or the Sandiaoling Waterfall Trail, both easily accessible from Taipei. These paths meander through lush landscapes and lead to stunning natural attractions, making them perfect for families and those seeking a more relaxed experience.

For seasoned hikers and thrill-seekers, Taiwan offers iconic trails like the Zhuilu Old Trail in

Taroko Gorge National Park. This heart-pounding trail snakes along narrow cliff faces, providing jaw-dropping views of the marble-walled gorge below. Another challenging option is tackling the formidable Jade Mountain (Yushan), the highest peak in Northeast Asia. The journey rewards hikers with stunning alpine scenery and a sense of accomplishment that's hard to match.

Taroko Gorge: A Hiker's Paradise

A crown jewel of Taiwan's hiking destinations, Taroko Gorge boasts a network of trails that wind through breathtaking landscapes of marble cliffs, rushing rivers, and verdant forests. Trails like the Shakadang Trail and Baiyang Waterfall Trail are relatively easy and suitable for families. For the more intrepid, the Zhuilu Old Trail offers an adrenaline-pumping experience, and the Dali–Cimu Trail takes you to hidden temples and serene natural wonders.

Alishan: Mystical Forest Treks

The Alishan National Scenic Area is renowned for its misty forests, ancient trees, and picturesque sunrise views. The Alishan Sacred Tree Trail is an excellent choice for those seeking an immersive forest experience, while the trails around the Alishan Train Station lead to serene viewpoints. Don't miss the opportunity to witness the "sea of clouds" phenomenon, where mist blankets the valleys in an ethereal display.

East Coast Trails: Coastal Beauty

Taiwan's east coast offers coastal trails that combine ocean views with rugged landscapes. The Bitou Cape Trail near Yilan showcases dramatic cliffs and ocean panoramas, while the Walami Trail in the East Rift Valley takes you deep into pristine forests, passing through indigenous communities and lush terrain.

Practical Tips for Hiking in Taiwan

1. Permits and Regulations: Some trails, especially in national parks, require permits. Check with local authorities and ensure you adhere to any regulations for a safe and respectful hiking experience.

2. Weather Preparedness: Taiwan's weather can change rapidly. Bring appropriate clothing and gear, including rainwear and sturdy hiking shoes.

3. Stay Hydrated and Snack Up: Carry sufficient water and energy snacks, especially on longer hikes where facilities might be limited.

4. Trail Information: Research trail conditions, difficulty levels, and any potential hazards before embarking on a hike.

5. Respect Nature and Culture: Leave no trace, follow established trails, and respect local customs and wildlife.

Taiwan's hiking and trekking options cater to adventurers seeking both physical challenges and spiritual connections with nature. The island's trails are not just pathways; they are gateways to a deeper understanding of Taiwan's natural wonders and cultural richness. So, pack your curiosity, determination, and a sense of wonder, and set off on an unforgettable journey through Taiwan's awe-inspiring landscapes.

- Cycling Routes

For cycling enthusiasts and outdoor adventurers, Taiwan presents a captivating playground of diverse landscapes, challenging terrains, and scenic routes that will leave you breathless in more ways than one. From coastal highways to mountain passes, the island offers a wide range of cycling experiences that cater to all skill levels. Strap on your helmet, hop on your bike, and get ready to explore some of the most exhilarating cycling routes Taiwan has to offer.

1. East Coast Scenic Route

Following the contours of Taiwan's stunning eastern coastline, the East Coast Scenic Route offers cyclists an unforgettable journey through rugged cliffs, crashing waves, and quaint fishing villages. The route stretches for over 170 kilometers, beginning in Hualien and winding its way down to Taitung. As you pedal along this route, you'll be treated to panoramic ocean views, lush greenery, and opportunities to interact with friendly locals.

2. Sun Moon Lake Loop

For a more leisurely cycling experience, the Sun Moon Lake Loop is an ideal choice. Circumnavigate the serene Sun Moon Lake, one of Taiwan's most picturesque destinations, and take in the breathtaking reflections of the surrounding mountains on the lake's tranquil waters. This approximately 30-kilometer route offers a mix of gentle slopes and flat stretches, making it perfect for cyclists of various fitness levels.

3. Taroko Gorge Challenge

Calling all thrill-seekers and experienced cyclists! The Taroko Gorge Challenge is a test of endurance and skill that takes you through the heart of Taroko National Park, renowned for its stunning marble cliffs and glistening rivers. The winding roads and steep climbs offer both a physical challenge and a reward of awe-inspiring views. This route demands a higher level of fitness and cycling proficiency, but the exhilaration of conquering the gorge's heights is unparalleled.

4. Taipei Riverside Paths

If you're looking for cycling routes within the cityscape, Taipei's extensive network of riverside paths is a delightful option. These well-maintained paths guide you along the banks of the Tamsui, Keelung, and Xindian rivers, allowing you to explore the urban landscape from a unique perspective. The paths are mostly flat and family-friendly, making them a great choice for travelers with children.

5. Coastal Highway 11

For those seeking a coastal adventure with a mix of charming villages and scenic coastline, Coastal Highway 11 delivers. Stretching along the northeastern coast, this route passes through sleepy towns, golden beaches, and dramatic cliffs. The relatively gentle terrain and refreshing sea breeze create a relaxed cycling experience that allows you to savor the beauty of Taiwan's eastern shores.

Preparation and Tips

Before embarking on your cycling journey in Taiwan, ensure you have the right equipment, such as a well-maintained bike, appropriate safety gear, and a good map or GPS device. Stay hydrated and energized by sampling local snacks and treats along the way. Additionally, familiarize yourself with local traffic rules and road conditions to ensure a safe and enjoyable ride.

With its diverse landscapes, welcoming culture, and well-constructed cycling infrastructure, Taiwan offers a cycling experience like no other. Whether you're seeking a leisurely ride along a tranquil lakeshore or an adrenaline-pumping challenge through mountainous terrain, Taiwan's cycling routes are ready to take you on an unforgettable adventure on two wheels.

- Water Sports

When it comes to aquatic adventures, Taiwan offers an enticing playground for water enthusiasts of all kinds. With its diverse coastline, crystal-clear waters, and a variety of aquatic ecosystems, the island beckons you to dive into a world of water sports that range from exhilarating to serene. Whether you're seeking heart-pounding action, serene relaxation, or a bit of both, Taiwan's waters have something for everyone.

Surfing and Windsurfing:
Taiwan's northern and eastern coastlines are a paradise for surfers and windsurfers. The northern beaches like Jinshan and Fulong offer excellent waves for surfers of all levels, from beginners to pros. On the windier east coast, Kenting and Green Bay are renowned for their world-class windsurfing conditions. Surf schools and rental shops abound, ensuring that both novices and experts can ride the waves.

Scuba Diving and Snorkeling:
Explore the mesmerizing underwater world surrounding Taiwan's shores. Pristine coral reefs,

vibrant marine life, and sunken shipwrecks are waiting to be discovered. Kenting National Park and the Green Island's Blue Cave are popular spots for both scuba diving and snorkeling, offering a chance to get up close and personal with marine creatures in their natural habitat.

Kayaking and Canoeing:
Taiwan's serene lakes and rivers provide excellent opportunities for kayaking and canoeing. Glide along the serene waters of Sun Moon Lake or explore the enchanting Liyu Lake. For a more adventurous experience, paddle through the lush gorges of the Taroko National Park. Whether you're a beginner or an experienced paddler, Taiwan's waterways offer diverse options for exploration.

Jet Skiing and Parasailing:
For those seeking an adrenaline rush, Taiwan's coastal destinations offer jet skiing and parasailing experiences. Kenting's clear waters and consistent winds make it a hotspot for these high-energy water sports. Feel the thrill as you zoom across the waves on a jet ski or soar above the ocean while parasailing, taking in breathtaking coastal views from a unique vantage point.

Stand-Up Paddleboarding (SUP):

SUP has gained popularity in Taiwan's tranquil bays and coves. The calm waters around Kenting and Penghu are perfect for beginners looking to master the art of balancing on a paddleboard. SUP not only provides a great workout but also offers a peaceful way to explore the coastline, bask in the sun, and relish the natural beauty that surrounds you.

Whitewater Rafting:
Venture into Taiwan's rugged interior for an exhilarating whitewater rafting experience. The Xiuguluan River is a favorite spot for thrill-seekers, offering challenging rapids set against the backdrop of lush landscapes. Join a guided rafting tour to navigate the twists and turns of these dynamic waterways, ensuring a safe and exciting adventure.

Whether you're a seasoned water sports enthusiast or looking to try something new, Taiwan's aquatic offerings promise unforgettable experiences. From the adrenaline-pumping thrills of surfing and jet skiing to the tranquil exploration of underwater worlds, the island's waters invite you to dive in and create lasting memories. With professional instructors, well-maintained equipment, and a breathtaking natural backdrop, Taiwan's water sports scene is a must-explore facet of your journey.

- *Paragliding and Skydiving*

For those seeking an adrenaline rush and a bird's-eye view of Taiwan's stunning landscapes, paragliding and skydiving offer unparalleled experiences that will leave you breathless in more ways than one. Taiwan's diverse terrain, ranging from majestic mountains to picturesque coastlines, provides the perfect backdrop for these exhilarating activities that let you touch the sky and feel the wind beneath your wings.

Paragliding: Glide Amidst Natural Splendor

Imagine floating gracefully in the air, carried by thermal currents, as you take in sweeping views of Taiwan's lush countryside or coastal panoramas. Paragliding in Taiwan offers a unique opportunity to connect with nature and experience the thrill of flight.

Top Paragliding Destinations:

1. Pingtung's Coastal Soar: The coastal areas near Pingtung, especially Kenting, offer paragliders the chance to take off from cliffs and soar over the turquoise waters of the Pacific Ocean. The combination of sea breeze and stunning landscapes

makes this region a favorite among both beginners and experienced paragliders.

2. Alishan Adventure: Alishan National Scenic Area's rolling hills and serene forests create a mesmerizing paragliding experience. Imagine launching from high elevations and gliding over lush landscapes, with a breathtaking view of the iconic Alishan sunrise.

3. Central Cross-Country Routes: Central Taiwan, including Taichung and Nantou, offers paragliding enthusiasts a chance to engage in cross-country flights. Soar over expansive fields, winding rivers, and quaint towns as you embark on thrilling paragliding journeys.

Skydiving: The Ultimate Leap of Faith

For the most daring adventurers, skydiving is the ultimate way to experience an adrenaline rush that's beyond compare. Plunging from thousands of feet above the ground, you'll feel the exhilaration of freefall before your parachute opens, offering a leisurely descent as you take in the breathtaking views below.

Top Skydiving Locations:

1. Taoyuan Skydiving Center: Located just outside Taipei, this center offers tandem skydiving experiences for beginners, where you're securely harnessed to an experienced instructor. You'll enjoy astonishing views of the city, coastline, and mountains during your descent.

2. Taitung's Coastal Dive: Skydiving over Taitung on the east coast offers a unique perspective of the Pacific Ocean meeting rugged cliffs. The sensation of freefall combined with the stunning vistas creates a memory you'll cherish forever.

3. Hualien's Aerial Majesty: Skydiving over Hualien allows you to marvel at the beauty of the Taroko Gorge National Park from an entirely new angle. The contrast of the emerald-green landscapes against the azure sky is simply breathtaking.

Practical Considerations:

- Safety First: Whether you're paragliding or skydiving, safety is paramount. Ensure that you choose reputable operators who adhere to international safety standards, provide thorough training, and use well-maintained equipment.

- Reservations: Both paragliding and skydiving experiences often require advance reservations, so plan ahead to secure your spot.

- Weather Factors: Activities are weather-dependent. Wind and weather conditions can affect the feasibility of paragliding and skydiving, so be prepared for possible rescheduling.

- Photography and Video: Many operators offer photography and video services to capture your thrilling moments, allowing you to relive your adventure and share it with friends and family.

For the adventurous at heart, paragliding and skydiving in Taiwan offer the chance to conquer the skies while taking in some of Asia's most breathtaking scenery. Whether you're a first-timer or a seasoned pro, these experiences promise unforgettable memories that will have you longing to return to the skies again and again.

Chapter 13. Thrilling Outdoor Destinations

- *Yushan National Park*

Nestled in the heart of Taiwan's central mountain range, Yushan National Park stands as a testament to the island's diverse natural beauty and striking landscapes. Renowned for its awe-inspiring alpine scenery, vibrant ecosystems, and challenging trekking trails, this national park is a must-visit destination for nature enthusiasts, hikers, and adventure seekers.

Key Highlights:

1. Mount Yushan (Jade Mountain): At the heart of the park stands Taiwan's highest peak, Mount Yushan, affectionately known as "Jade Mountain." With an elevation of 3,952 meters (12,966 feet), reaching the summit is a bucket-list achievement for many hikers. The journey offers ever-changing vistas, from lush forests to rugged terrain, making it an unforgettable experience.

2. Diverse Flora and Fauna: Yushan National Park boasts a rich array of plant and animal species, many of which are endemic to Taiwan. The park's ecosystems shift dramatically with altitude, showcasing everything from subtropical rainforests

to alpine meadows. The Formosan black bear, Mikado pheasant, and various species of rhododendron are just a few of the park's unique inhabitants.

3. Trails and Hiking Routes: The park offers a range of hiking trails suitable for different levels of experience. The most famous trail is the Yushan Main Peak Trail, leading to the summit of Jade Mountain. This demanding trek rewards hikers with breathtaking vistas and a profound sense of accomplishment. Other trails, such as the Siyuan Trail and Batongguan Historic Trail, provide diverse landscapes and insights into Taiwan's history.

4. Seven Major Peaks: Beyond Jade Mountain, Yushan National Park features six other major peaks, each offering a distinctive trekking experience. These peaks include East Yushan, South Yushan, North Yushan, and more. Adventurous hikers can challenge themselves by conquering multiple peaks over a longer expedition.

5. Scenic Beauty: Yushan's landscapes are truly captivating. Visitors can marvel at stunning sunrise and sunset views from the mountaintops, and during clear nights, the stargazing opportunities are

unparalleled. Alpine lakes, deep valleys, and dramatic ridges create a picturesque backdrop for every step of the journey.

6. Permits and Regulations: Due to its popularity and the need for environmental protection, hikers must obtain permits to access certain areas of the park, particularly for the Jade Mountain Main Peak Trail. The park authority carefully manages visitor numbers to preserve the delicate ecosystems and provide a safe experience.

7. Planning and Preparation: Proper preparation is essential for a successful Yushan trek. Hikers should be physically fit, equipped with appropriate clothing and gear, and have a clear understanding of the trail they plan to tackle. Hiring a local guide can greatly enhance the experience, ensuring safety and providing valuable insights.

Yushan National Park encapsulates the soul of Taiwan's natural beauty, offering a rare chance to immerse yourself in stunning landscapes, embrace the thrill of adventure, and witness the resilience of life at high altitudes. Whether you're a dedicated hiker or simply seeking a connection with nature, Yushan's alpine wonderland promises an unforgettable journey that will leave you in awe of Taiwan's remarkable natural heritage.

- *Kenting National Park*

Nestled at the southern tip of Taiwan, Kenting National Park stands as a mesmerizing testament to the island's natural beauty. With its stunning coastline, lush landscapes, and vibrant ecosystems, this park offers an escape into a tropical wonderland that appeals to a wide range of travelers.

1. Natural Diversity and Ecological Marvels

Kenting National Park is a haven of biodiversity, encompassing a variety of landscapes from dense forests to coral reefs. The park's ecosystems are home to numerous plant and animal species, some of which are found nowhere else on Earth. The diverse habitats provide a haven for wildlife enthusiasts and nature lovers.

2. Pristine Beaches and Crystal Waters

The park boasts some of Taiwan's most alluring beaches, with soft white sands meeting the azure waters of the Pacific Ocean. Visitors can unwind under the sun, take a leisurely swim, or engage in water activities such as snorkeling and diving to explore the vibrant underwater world. Baisha Bay and Nanwan Beach are popular spots for relaxation and recreation.

3. Eluanbi Lighthouse: A Symbol of Resilience

Standing proudly against the backdrop of Kenting's dramatic coastline is the iconic Eluanbi Lighthouse. This historic structure, perched atop rugged cliffs, has served as a guardian of the seas for over a century. Visitors can explore the lighthouse, learn about its history, and savor panoramic views of the surrounding landscape.

4. Rich Cultural Heritage

Kenting isn't just about natural beauty; it also carries a rich cultural heritage. The indigenous cultures of the region are celebrated through traditional arts, crafts, and performances. The nearby Hengchun Old Town, with its well-preserved city walls and historic architecture, offers a glimpse into Taiwan's colonial past.

5. Hiking and Outdoor Adventures

For those seeking active pursuits, Kenting offers a plethora of hiking trails that wind through forests, cliffs, and coastal paths. The famous Maobitou Trail offers breathtaking views of the rugged shoreline, while the Longpan Park Trail presents expansive vistas of the ocean meeting the sky.

6. Night Markets and Culinary Delights

Kenting's night markets are a treasure trove of local flavors. Indulge in a gastronomic adventure as you sample delectable street food, from seafood skewers to traditional desserts. The local seafood is a highlight, freshly caught from the surrounding waters.

7. Conservation and Sustainability

The park's management places a strong emphasis on conservation and sustainability. Visitors are encouraged to explore responsibly, respecting the delicate ecosystems and local communities. Participation in beach clean-up events and other eco-friendly activities is highly encouraged.

8. Best Time to Visit

Kenting's tropical climate ensures warm temperatures throughout the year. The peak tourist season falls between October and April when the weather is pleasant and dry, making it an ideal time for outdoor activities and exploration.

9. Getting There

Kenting National Park is easily accessible from major cities like Kaohsiung and Taitung. Bus services connect these cities to the park, providing a convenient option for travelers. Renting a scooter or car is also popular for exploring the park at your own pace.

A visit to Kenting National Park offers an opportunity to experience the beauty and diversity that define Taiwan's southern coastline. Whether you're an adventure seeker, a nature enthusiast, or someone seeking a tranquil escape, this tropical paradise promises an unforgettable journey into the heart of Taiwan's natural splendor.

- *Green Island*

Nestled in the vast blue expanse of the Pacific Ocean, Green Island (綠島) stands as a tiny emerald jewel in Taiwan's maritime crown. This alluring destination is a must-visit for travelers seeking both natural wonders and historical insights. With its crystal-clear waters, lush landscapes, and intriguing history, Green Island offers an unforgettable experience that captures the essence of Taiwan's diverse offerings.

Natural Beauty:
Green Island boasts breathtaking natural beauty that appeals to nature enthusiasts and adventurers alike. From its pristine beaches to rugged coastlines and dense forests, the island's landscapes provide a range of outdoor activities and sights to explore:

1. Beaches and Snorkeling: The island's shores are fringed with beaches offering powdery white sands and azure waters. The most famous, and arguably the most beautiful, is Nanliao Beach. Snorkeling and diving enthusiasts are treated to vibrant coral reefs teeming with marine life just off the coast.

2. Underwater Hot Springs: One of Green Island's unique features is its underwater hot springs. Snorkelers and divers can experience the surreal sensation of soaking in warm, mineral-rich water amid the ocean waves.

3. Ludao Lighthouse: Perched on a cliff overlooking the sea, Ludao Lighthouse offers panoramic views

of the island's dramatic coastline. The lighthouse itself is an iconic symbol of Green Island.

Historical Significance:
Beyond its natural beauty, Green Island also holds a significant place in Taiwan's history:

1. Former Political Prison:
   During Taiwan's martial law period, Green Island was home to a political prison. Visitors can explore the Green Island Human Rights Culture Park, which sheds light on the island's history as a place of incarceration and the struggles of political prisoners.

2. Hai'an Road: This winding coastal road showcases remnants of the island's history, including the remains of guard towers and prison facilities. The road offers spectacular views and poignant reminders of the past.

Getting There:
Reaching Green Island involves a ferry ride or a short flight from Taiwan's eastern coast. The island's small size makes it easy to explore by scooter, bicycle, or even on foot.

Best Time to Visit:

The ideal time to explore Green Island is during the spring and fall months, from March to May and September to November, when the weather is pleasant and the sea conditions are favorable for water activities.

Accommodation:
Green Island offers a range of accommodation options, from guesthouses and homestays to more upscale resorts. Visitors can choose accommodations that suit their preferences and budget.

In summary, Green Island is a captivating destination that seamlessly weaves natural beauty and historical significance. Whether you're an adventure seeker, a history buff, or simply a traveler in search of unique experiences, this emerald paradise is sure to leave an indelible mark on your journey through Taiwan.

- Maolin National Scenic Area

Nestled in the southern part of Taiwan, the Maolin National Scenic Area is a hidden paradise for nature enthusiasts, adventure seekers, and those looking to experience the beauty of Taiwan's lush landscapes. This unique destination offers a captivating blend of dense forests, stunning waterfalls, indigenous culture, and adrenaline-pumping activities.

Natural Splendor:
The Maolin National Scenic Area is renowned for its breathtaking landscapes. Verdant mountains, pristine rivers, and cascading waterfalls create a picturesque backdrop that's perfect for hiking, photography, and serene contemplation. The area is particularly famous for its annual Purple Butterfly Valley phenomenon, where thousands of purple butterflies gather, adding a touch of magic to the already awe-inspiring surroundings.

Hot Springs Haven:
Within the scenic area, you'll find the Maolin Hot Springs, a rejuvenating oasis for travelers. These natural hot springs are believed to have therapeutic properties, and soaking in their mineral-rich waters is a soothing experience. Surrounded by lush greenery, these hot springs provide a relaxing retreat after a day of exploration.

Indigenous Culture:
The Maolin area is home to the Rukai indigenous people, who have maintained their unique traditions and way of life for generations. Visitors have the opportunity to engage with the local

community, learning about their customs, art, and traditional rituals. The Rukai Cultural Village offers insights into their rich heritage, and you can even participate in workshops to create traditional crafts.

Adventurous Activities:
For thrill-seekers, Maolin offers a range of adventure activities. The area's rugged terrain is perfect for hiking and trekking, with trails catering to various skill levels. The adventurous can tackle the famous Wanshan Great Trail, which provides panoramic views of the surrounding mountains. Additionally, Maolin offers opportunities for river tracing, abseiling down waterfalls, and even paragliding, offering a heart-pounding and breathtaking perspective of the landscape.

Best Time to Visit:
The Maolin National Scenic Area is an all-season destination, each offering a distinct charm. Spring and summer (April to August) are great for vibrant flora, while fall (September to November) provides a stunning mix of colors as leaves change. Winter (December to February) offers a tranquil atmosphere, with the bonus of the Purple Butterfly Valley phenomenon in February and March.

Getting There:

Maolin is accessible from Kaohsiung City, one of Taiwan's major cities. You can take a bus or drive, with the journey offering its own scenic delights. It's recommended to check the latest transportation options and schedules before your visit.

For those looking to immerse themselves in Taiwan's natural beauty, cultural heritage, and outdoor adventures, the Maolin National Scenic Area promises an unforgettable experience. Whether you're a nature lover, an adventure enthusiast, or someone seeking tranquility away from the city, Maolin invites you to explore its hidden treasures and create lasting memories in the heart of Taiwan's southern wilderness.

Chapter 14. Taiwanese Cuisine

- *Must-Try Dishes*

Taiwan is a paradise for food lovers, where the streets come alive with the aroma of sizzling woks, and bustling night markets offer a tantalizing array of culinary delights. From savory to sweet, traditional to modern, the island's diverse food scene reflects its rich cultural history and innovative spirit. Here are some must-try dishes that will undoubtedly delight your taste buds during your visit to Taiwan:

1. Beef Noodle Soup (牛肉麵)
A beloved Taiwanese classic, beef noodle soup is a hearty and flavorful dish that showcases the island's culinary prowess. Tender chunks of beef simmered in a robust broth infused with spices and herbs are served over chewy noodles. Whether you prefer a rich, spicy broth or a clear, aromatic one, a steaming bowl of beef noodle soup is a culinary experience not to be missed.

2. Xiao Long Bao (小籠包)
These delicate soup dumplings have gained international fame, and for good reason. Xiao long bao are delicate, handcrafted dumplings filled with a mixture of savory broth and minced pork or other

fillings. Carefully pleated, they are steamed to perfection, resulting in a burst of flavors and aromas with every bite. Dip them in a combination of soy sauce, vinegar, and ginger for an unforgettable taste sensation.

3. Oyster Omelette (蚵仔煎)
A popular street food item, oyster omelette combines plump, succulent oysters with a crispy, eggy batter. Pan-fried to perfection and often served with a tangy sweet sauce, this dish offers a delightful mix of textures and flavors – a true taste of Taiwanese comfort food.

4. Stinky Tofu (臭豆腐)
An acquired taste that's adored by locals and adventurous eaters alike, stinky tofu lives up to its name in terms of aroma. However, the strong scent belies its delicious taste. Available in various forms – deep-fried, grilled, or braised – stinky tofu is crispy on the outside and tender on the inside. Don't let its reputation deter you; this dish offers a unique and unforgettable culinary experience.

5. Bubble Tea (珍珠奶茶)
Originating in Taiwan, bubble tea (also known as boba tea) has become a global sensation. This refreshing drink features a base of milk tea or fruit

tea, typically sweetened, and is adorned with chewy tapioca pearls that add a delightful texture. Customize your drink by choosing the level of sweetness and ice, and discover why bubble tea has captured the hearts of so many.

6. Gua Bao (割包)

Gua bao, also known as "Taiwanese hamburger," is a snack-sized steamed bun filled with tender, braised pork belly, pickled mustard greens, and ground peanuts. The combination of flavors and textures – the richness of the pork, the crunch of the greens, and the nutty, sweet undertones – creates a harmonious and satisfying dish.

7. Pineapple Cake (鳳梨酥)

For those with a sweet tooth, Taiwan's pineapple cakes are a treat not to be missed. These buttery pastries are filled with sweet pineapple jam, creating a balanced blend of flavors. Often presented as gifts or souvenirs, these delectable treats encapsulate the essence of Taiwanese hospitality.

As you embark on your culinary journey through Taiwan, these dishes represent just a glimpse into the diverse and exciting world of Taiwanese cuisine. Each bite tells a story of tradition, innovation, and a deep appreciation for the art of cooking. So, dive into the local eateries, explore the bustling night markets, and savor every moment as you savor these must-try dishes that are an integral part of Taiwan's cultural tapestry.

- *Night Markets and Street Food*

One of the most exhilarating and unforgettable experiences you'll have in Taiwan is exploring its vibrant night markets and indulging in its tantalizing street food offerings. These lively hubs of culinary delight are not just about eating; they're a sensory journey that immerses you in the heart and soul of Taiwanese culture.

Night Market Extravaganza

Night markets are an integral part of Taiwanese urban life, bustling with energy and drawing both locals and visitors into a world of endless stalls, neon lights, and a symphony of scents. Each market has its unique character, reflecting the local community and its traditions. Taipei's Shilin Night Market, Raohe Street Night Market, and Tainan's Garden Night Market are just a few of the iconic ones that offer an array of experiences.

A Culinary Playground

The heart of Taiwan's night markets lies in their street food stalls, where culinary artisans craft dishes that range from traditional to innovative, all bursting with flavor. The beauty of street food lies in its accessibility – you can sample a multitude of dishes in a single evening, making it a true culinary adventure.

Must-Try Taiwanese Street Food

1. Stinky Tofu: A polarizing but quintessential Taiwanese dish. Its pungent aroma disguises its delectable taste.

2. Xiao Long Bao: These delicate soup dumplings are filled with flavorful broth and tender meat, creating a burst of taste with every bite.

3. Oyster Omelette: A harmonious mix of eggs, oysters, and vegetables, this dish is a comforting and flavorful delight.

4. Bubble Tea: Originating in Taiwan, this globally adored drink features tapioca pearls submerged in a variety of sweet teas and milk.

5. Gua Bao: Also known as the Taiwanese burger, this snack consists of braised pork belly, peanuts, cilantro, and pickled vegetables in a fluffy steamed bun.

6. Scallion Pancakes: These crispy and savory pancakes are a popular snack, often served with a variety of fillings and sauces.

7. Fried Chicken Cutlet: A beloved street food, the chicken cutlet is seasoned, breaded, and fried to crispy perfection.

Navigating the Night Markets

As you explore the vibrant labyrinth of stalls, be prepared to embrace the crowds, the lively chatter, and the constant sizzle of woks. Engage with local vendors, try new flavors, and follow your nose to discover hidden gems. While cash is preferred, some vendors are now accepting electronic payments.

Tips for an Enjoyable Experience

- Come Hungry: The variety can be overwhelming, so arrive with an empty stomach and a curious palate.

- Share and Sample: Gather a group of fellow travelers to share and sample dishes, allowing you to try more.
- Observe Locals: Watch what locals are eating – it's a good indicator of what's particularly delicious.
- Hydrate: Don't forget to stay hydrated amidst all the eating. Fruit juices and herbal teas are often available.
- Open Mind, Open Heart: Be open to trying new things; you might discover a new favorite dish.

Exploring night markets and indulging in street food is not just about satisfying your taste buds – it's about immersing yourself in Taiwan's dynamic culture, forging connections with locals, and creating memories that will linger long after you've left. So, step into the world of aromas, flavors, and sounds, and let Taiwan's night markets weave their enchanting spell over you.

- Tea Culture

No exploration of Taiwan is complete without delving into its rich and storied tea culture. Renowned as one of the world's top tea producers, Taiwan's rolling hills and temperate climate provide the perfect environment for cultivating some of the finest teas you'll ever encounter. Beyond being a mere beverage, tea in Taiwan is an art form, a cultural tradition, and a way of life that invites you to savor both the flavors and the tranquility it brings.

A Brief History of Taiwanese Tea

Tea has been an integral part of Taiwanese culture for centuries, with a history dating back to the 17th century. The island's unique geography and climatic conditions have nurtured the growth of various tea varieties, each reflecting the distinct qualities of the region it's grown in. From the mist-covered highlands to the fertile valleys, Taiwan's diverse landscapes yield teas that are prized for their aroma, flavor, and health benefits.

Tea Varieties and Regions

Taiwan boasts a remarkable range of tea types, each celebrated for its unique characteristics. The island is particularly famous for its oolong teas, which undergo intricate processing to achieve their distinct flavors and aromas. Some of the most notable oolong varieties include:

- High Mountain Oolong: Grown at elevations of over 1,000 meters, these teas are known for their floral fragrances, delicate tastes, and smooth

finishes. The Alishan and Lishan regions are renowned for producing exceptional high mountain oolongs.
- Dong Ding Oolong: Hailing from the central mountains, these teas offer a balance of floral and roasted notes, often described as having a captivating "nong xiang" aroma.
- Iron Goddess of Mercy (Tie Guan Yin): With roots in Fujian, China, this tea variety has been lovingly embraced by Taiwan. Its sweet and floral taste is a favorite among many tea enthusiasts.

Tea Houses and Ceremonies

Exploring Taiwan's tea culture often involves visiting traditional tea houses, where the art of tea preparation is practiced with precision and grace. Here, you can experience Gongfu Cha, a ceremonial method of preparing tea that emphasizes multiple short steepings to extract the full range of flavors from the leaves.

Local tea masters will guide you through the process, showcasing the delicate balance between tea leaves, water temperature, and steeping time. The act of pouring and sharing tea becomes a meditative experience, fostering a deep connection with the moment and your companions.

Tea Tourism and Experiences

For travelers seeking a deeper dive into Taiwan's tea culture, there are numerous opportunities to visit tea plantations and witness the harvesting and processing stages firsthand. Many regions, such as Maokong in Taipei or the Pinglin District in New Taipei City, offer guided tours that unveil the intricate journey from leaf to cup.

Whether you're sipping tea while gazing at mist-shrouded mountains or partaking in a traditional tea ceremony, Taiwan's tea culture invites you to slow down, embrace mindfulness, and appreciate the simple beauty of a well-steeped cup.

Bringing a Piece of Taiwan Home

As you bid farewell to Taiwan, consider taking a piece of its tea culture with you. From the bustling night markets to specialty tea shops, you'll find an array of teas – packaged with care and adorned with the essence of Taiwan's landscapes – to enjoy long after your journey has ended. Whether you're a connoisseur or a casual tea drinker, the flavors and memories of Taiwan's tea culture will linger in your heart and cup, reminding you of the serenity and tradition you discovered on this remarkable island.

Chapter 15. Dining Experiences

- *Traditional Restaurants*

Venturing into Taiwan's culinary landscape means stepping back in time to savor authentic flavors that have been lovingly preserved through generations. The island's traditional restaurants offer not just a meal, but an immersive experience into its rich history and cultural heritage. From age-old recipes passed down through families to charming settings that transport you to another era, these establishments are a must-visit for those seeking a genuine taste of Taiwan.

1. Teahouses and Dim Sum Eateries

Taiwan's tea houses are more than just places to enjoy a cup of tea – they're windows into the island's cultural soul. These serene sanctuaries offer a variety of teas, each accompanied by a delectable selection of dim sum, or small savory and sweet dishes. As you sip on fragrant oolong tea, indulge in mouthwatering dumplings, pastries, and delicate bites that harmonize with the tranquil ambiance.

2. Mazu Temples and Seafood Restaurants

In coastal towns, especially those with strong fishing traditions, you'll often find traditional restaurants nestled near Mazu temples. These eateries serve up freshly caught seafood that pays homage to the sea goddess Mazu. Feast on dishes like braised fish, squid, crab, and prawns prepared with a mix of age-old techniques and innovative flavors, all while immersed in the sea's whispers and the temple's mystique.

3. Old-Style Noodle Shops

Taiwan's noodle culture is steeped in history, with traditional noodle shops preserving the essence of generations past. Step into a modest shop, where skilled noodle artisans craft strands of goodness right before your eyes. Whether you opt for beef noodle soup, minced pork noodles, or a bowl of danzai noodles, you're tasting a slice of Taiwan's culinary heritage that's been perfected over time.

4. Lu Rou Fan and Braised Delights

Lu rou fan, or braised pork rice, is a Taiwanese comfort food that speaks to the soul. In traditional restaurants, you'll find versions of this dish that hark back to family recipes cooked with love and attention. The tender, succulent pork belly is slowly braised in aromatic spices, creating a harmonious balance of flavors that's served over a bed of steamed rice – a satisfying experience that transcends mere sustenance.

5. Historical Eateries in Old Quarters

Taiwan's older neighborhoods are home to eateries that have stood the test of time, serving as culinary time capsules. These establishments, often tucked into alleyways and side streets, transport you to a different era with their vintage decor and nostalgic ambiance. From iconic breakfast joints offering soy milk and savory Chinese crullers to hole-in-the-wall noodle shops, these places resonate with the echoes of generations past.

6. Indigenous Cuisine Gatherings

For a truly authentic taste of Taiwan's diverse heritage, seek out restaurants that celebrate indigenous cuisine. These eateries showcase the flavors of Taiwan's aboriginal communities, utilizing locally sourced ingredients and ancient cooking techniques. Savor dishes like millet wine chicken, bamboo rice, and wild boar, while learning about the stories and traditions that shape indigenous culture.

7. Yan Su Ji and Traditional Snacks

Yan su ji, or salt and pepper chicken, is a beloved Taiwanese snack that embodies the island's culinary charm. Visit traditional stalls or small eateries that specialize in this finger-licking delight. Crispy on the outside, tender on the inside, each bite of this seasoned chicken takes you on a journey through the bustling streets of Taiwan's night markets.

Immerse Yourself in Tradition

When you dine at Taiwan's traditional restaurants, you're not just indulging your taste buds – you're immersing yourself in the heart and soul of the island's culture. From ancient teahouses to rustic seafood eateries, these culinary treasures offer more than meals; they're invitations to step into Taiwan's past and savor the authenticity that defines its gastronomic heritage. So, embark on a culinary journey through time, and let the flavors of tradition leave an indelible mark on your taste memories.

- *Night Market Food Tours*

When the sun sets and the neon lights begin to dance, Taiwan's night markets come alive, offering an irresistible invitation to indulge in a sensory journey through the country's rich culinary landscape. Night market food tours are not just about eating; they're about immersing yourself in the heart of Taiwanese culture, where flavors, aromas, and bustling atmospheres combine to create an unforgettable experience.

Exploring Taiwan's Culinary Tapestry

Night markets are the beating heart of Taiwanese food culture, where locals and visitors alike gather to savor traditional dishes, sample innovative street eats, and enjoy the camaraderie of communal dining. These markets are a treasure trove of gastronomic delights, a feast for both the stomach and the senses.

The Sights and Sounds of Night Market Magic

As you embark on a night market food tour, you'll find yourself navigating through a labyrinth of stalls that spill over with color, aroma, and energy. Stalls adorned with bright signage beckon you to explore further, offering a dizzying array of culinary options that range from iconic street food classics to modern fusions.

Must-Try Night Market Delights

No night market food tour is complete without indulging in some of Taiwan's most beloved dishes. Sink your teeth into the fluffy and savory sensation of a giant crispy chicken cutlet, or savor the delicate flavors of xiao long bao, soup dumplings bursting with delectable fillings. Adventure seekers might even try stinky tofu, a polarizing dish that's become a badge of honor for those who dare.

A Gastronomic Adventure for All Tastes

Night markets are not just for the daring eaters. They offer a range of options to suit every palate. Nibble on skewers of fresh fruit coated in tangy tamarind sauce or sample local sweets like pineapple cakes and mochi. Vegetarians and vegans will also find a surprising variety of plant-based options, from tofu-based dishes to vegetable-stuffed spring rolls.

Beyond the Palate: Cultural Insights

The night market food tour isn't just about food; it's a window into Taiwan's culture and way of life. Engage with friendly vendors, many of whom have perfected their recipes over generations. Discover the stories behind local specialties and learn about the culinary techniques that have been passed down through the ages.

Practical Tips for Your Night Market Food Tour

1. Come Hungry: Night markets offer an abundance of options, so arrive with an empty stomach and a sense of adventure.

2. Cash is King: While some stalls may accept cards, it's best to have cash on hand, as it's the most widely accepted form of payment.

3. Exploring with a Guide: Consider joining a guided night market food tour to gain deeper insights, local recommendations, and insider knowledge.

4. Dress Comfortably: Night markets can get crowded and busy, so wear comfortable shoes and clothing that can withstand a little food spillage.

5. Embrace the Chaos: Night markets can be bustling and noisy, but that's part of the charm. Embrace the vibrant atmosphere and dive in.

A night market food tour in Taiwan is more than a culinary adventure – it's a cultural experience that connects you with the heart and soul of the country. Through the scents, tastes, and stories shared within these lively markets, you'll not only discover the essence of Taiwanese cuisine but also forge unforgettable memories that will linger long after your journey ends. So, let the night markets guide you on a delicious exploration of Taiwan's vibrant food scene, one bite at a time.

- Cooking Classes

No journey to Taiwan is complete without diving into its vibrant culinary scene, and what better way to do so than by taking part in a cooking class? Immerse yourself in the heart of Taiwanese gastronomy as you learn to craft delectable dishes under the guidance of skilled local chefs. These cooking classes offer not only a hands-on experience but also a deeper connection to the island's culture, traditions, and flavors.

Discover Local Ingredients and Techniques

Taiwanese cuisine is a harmonious blend of influences from China, Japan, Southeast Asia, and indigenous cultures. Taking a cooking class in Taiwan offers you the chance to explore the unique ingredients that form the foundation of these mouthwatering dishes. From fragrant herbs and exotic spices to fresh seafood and seasonal vegetables, you'll discover the secrets behind creating the intricate flavors that define Taiwanese cuisine.

The Joy of Interactive Learning

Cooking classes in Taiwan are more than just culinary lessons – they are interactive experiences that engage all your senses. Whether you're a seasoned home cook or a novice in the kitchen, the patient and passionate instructors will guide you through each step, helping you understand the techniques behind preparing signature dishes. From hand-rolling spring rolls to perfecting the art of making beef noodle soup, every class is an opportunity to enhance your culinary skills.

A Glimpse into Local Life

Participating in a cooking class is like opening a window into the daily life of locals. As you shop for ingredients at bustling markets, chat with vendors, and prepare dishes in a traditional kitchen, you'll gain insights into the cultural nuances that shape Taiwanese cuisine. These classes often foster a sense of camaraderie as you bond with fellow participants, sharing stories and laughter over a shared love for food.

Cooking Classes for Every Taste

Taiwan offers a diverse array of cooking classes to suit various preferences and dietary requirements. Whether you're interested in mastering the art of crafting delicate dumplings, creating the famous bubble milk tea, or learning to cook sumptuous seafood feasts, there's a class to cater to every palate.

Memories and Skills to Take Home

One of the most rewarding aspects of joining a cooking class in Taiwan is that the experience doesn't end with the class itself. Armed with newfound culinary skills and recipes, you can recreate the flavors of Taiwan in your own kitchen back home. Each bite will transport you back to the vibrant markets, the sizzling woks, and the warm-hearted instructors who shared their culinary wisdom with you.

Practical Information

- Booking: It's advisable to book cooking classes in advance, either directly with the cooking school or through reputable travel agencies.

- Duration: Cooking classes typically last a few hours to half a day, allowing for a comprehensive culinary experience.

- Locations: Classes are offered in major cities like Taipei, Kaohsiung, and Tainan, as well as in more rural areas where you can learn traditional indigenous cooking methods.

- Language: Many cooking schools offer classes in English, making it accessible to international visitors.

- Group Sizes: Classes can range from intimate sessions to larger groups, so you can choose the setting that suits your preference.

As you embark on your culinary journey through Taiwan, let the aromas, flavors, and techniques you encounter in these cooking classes become cherished souvenirs of your time on the island. Whether you're traveling solo, with a partner, or as a family, a cooking class offers a truly immersive and delightful way to connect with Taiwan's rich food culture.

Chapter 16. Packing Guide

- *Weather-Appropriate Clothing*

Taiwan's climate is as diverse as its landscapes, and each season brings its own unique charm to this island paradise. When it comes to packing your bags, understanding the weather patterns and dressing appropriately is key to enjoying your trip to the fullest. From the warmth of summer to the crispness of winter, here's a guide on what to wear in Taiwan throughout the year.

Spring (March to May):
Spring is a delightful time to explore Taiwan. As the weather starts to warm up, you'll want to pack a mix of light layers. Opt for breathable fabrics like cotton and linen, along with comfortable walking shoes for your city strolls and nature hikes. A light jacket or cardigan will come in handy for cooler evenings, especially in the northern and central parts of the island. Don't forget to bring an umbrella or a rain jacket, as occasional showers are common during this season.

Summer (June to August):
Summer in Taiwan can be hot and humid, so it's all about staying cool and comfortable. Lightweight, loose-fitting clothing is your best bet. Think shorts,

skirts, tank tops, and short-sleeved shirts. Sunscreen, a wide-brimmed hat, and sunglasses are essential to protect yourself from the strong sun. Don't forget to carry a refillable water bottle to stay hydrated while you explore the bustling streets or lounge on the sun-soaked beaches.

Autumn (September to November):
Autumn is arguably the most pleasant time to visit Taiwan. The humidity drops, and the weather becomes milder. Pack a mix of short-sleeved and long-sleeved shirts, along with a light jacket or sweater for the cooler evenings. It's also a good idea to have a light rain jacket or umbrella on hand, as occasional showers can still occur. Don't forget to include comfortable walking shoes, as autumn is a great time to explore the outdoors and embark on scenic hikes.

Winter (December to February):
Winter in Taiwan varies by region, with northern areas experiencing cooler temperatures than the south. In northern Taiwan, layers are your best friend. Pack warm sweaters, long-sleeved shirts, and a medium-weight jacket. If you're heading to the mountains or more northern destinations, consider bringing a heavier coat. In the southern parts of Taiwan, you can get away with lighter

layers, but it's still a good idea to have a sweater or jacket for cooler evenings.

Special Considerations:
- Rain Gear: Taiwan's weather can be unpredictable, so it's wise to pack an umbrella or a compact rain jacket no matter the season.
- Comfortable Shoes: Regardless of the season, comfortable walking shoes are a must. You'll likely be exploring a lot on foot, so make sure your footwear is both supportive and suitable for various terrains.
- Modesty in Temples: If you plan to visit temples, remember to dress modestly. This usually means covering your shoulders and knees. Carrying a scarf or a shawl to drape over your shoulders can be a convenient way to respect temple etiquette.

By tailoring your wardrobe to the specific season you're visiting, you'll not only be comfortable but also ready to fully immerse yourself in Taiwan's natural beauty, rich culture, and vibrant cities, regardless of the weather.

- Essentials Checklist

Preparing for your journey to Taiwan involves a careful consideration of both the destination's unique characteristics and your personal needs. This essentials checklist has been crafted to ensure that you pack smartly and comfortably, allowing you to fully enjoy your adventure on this captivating island.

1. Clothing:
- Light and Breathable Clothing: Taiwan's climate is generally humid and subtropical, so opt for lightweight fabrics to stay comfortable in the heat.
- Rain Gear: Depending on the season, occasional rain showers are common. Pack a compact umbrella or a lightweight rain jacket.
- Comfortable Walking Shoes: With numerous attractions and outdoor activities, comfortable walking shoes are a must. Sneakers or sturdy sandals are recommended.
- Swimwear: If you plan to visit the beaches or hot springs, don't forget to pack your swimwear.

2. Weather-Appropriate Attire:
- Sun Protection: Bring sunglasses, a wide-brimmed hat, and sunscreen to shield yourself from Taiwan's strong sun.
- Warm Clothing: For higher elevations and cooler seasons, pack a light sweater or jacket.

3. Electronics:

- Universal Travel Adapter: Taiwan uses Type A and Type B sockets, so make sure your electronics can be charged with these plug types.
- Power Bank: To keep your devices charged on the go.

4. Travel Documents:
- Passport and Visa: Ensure your passport is valid for at least six months beyond your intended stay. Check visa requirements before traveling.
- Printed Copies: Have physical copies of important documents like your passport, travel insurance, hotel reservations, and emergency contacts.

5. Health and Personal Care:
- Prescription Medications: If you take any medications, bring an ample supply for the duration of your trip.
- Basic First Aid Kit: Include items like adhesive bandages, antiseptic wipes, pain relievers, and any specific medications you might need.
- Insect Repellent: Especially useful in rural areas.
- Toiletries: Pack your essentials, including toothbrush, toothpaste, soap, shampoo, and any special personal care items.
- Hand Sanitizer: Useful for staying clean on the go.

6. Miscellaneous:

- Reusable Water Bottle: Tap water in Taiwan is generally safe to drink, so having a reusable water bottle will help you stay hydrated.
- Backpack or Day Bag: For carrying your essentials during day trips and sightseeing.
- Local Currency: Taiwanese New Dollar (TWD). Carry some local cash for smaller vendors and places that might not accept cards.
- Language Guide or Translation App: While many locals speak English, having some basic local phrases can enhance your experience.

7. Important Reminders:
- Check Weather Forecasts: Taiwan's weather can vary, so keep an eye on forecasts to pack accordingly.
- Pack Lightly: Laundry facilities are often available, so you can pack fewer clothes and do laundry if needed.
- Respect Local Culture: Taiwan is respectful of modest dressing, especially in religious sites. Consider packing clothing that covers your shoulders and knees for such visits.

Remember that your packing list might vary based on your travel style and the specific regions you plan to explore. With this essential checklist as your guide, you'll be well-equipped to make the most of your Taiwan adventure, ensuring comfort, convenience, and unforgettable memories.

Chapter 17. Communication and Connectivity

- *SIM Cards and Wi-Fi Access*

Staying connected while exploring the enchanting landscapes and vibrant cities of Taiwan is essential for a smooth and enjoyable travel experience. Luckily, Taiwan offers a range of options for acquiring SIM cards and accessing Wi-Fi, ensuring you're always just a click away from maps, translations, and sharing your incredible moments with the world.

1. SIM Cards: Unveil Seamless Connectivity

Getting a local SIM card in Taiwan is a hassle-free way to enjoy uninterrupted connectivity. Upon your arrival at major airports, you'll find kiosks and stores offering a variety of prepaid SIM card options catering to different data needs and durations. These cards typically provide high-speed data, local minutes, and sometimes even international calls, ensuring you can stay in touch with loved ones and navigate the country with ease.

2. Popular Telecom Operators

Taiwan boasts several reputable telecom operators that offer reliable SIM card options:

- Chunghwa Telecom: The largest telecom operator in Taiwan, offering extensive coverage across the island.

- FarEasTone: Known for its excellent network coverage and customer service.

- Taiwan Mobile: Provides a range of prepaid SIM options with good network coverage.

3. Wi-Fi Access: Staying Connected on the Go

Wi-Fi connectivity is widely available throughout Taiwan, making it easy to stay connected while exploring. Many hotels, cafes, restaurants, and tourist attractions offer free Wi-Fi access. You can also find Wi-Fi hotspots in major transportation hubs like train stations and airports.

4. iPass: Island-Wide Wi-Fi Access

iPass is a convenient service that offers island-wide Wi-Fi access. It allows you to connect to Wi-Fi networks at thousands of locations, including hotels, restaurants, and public areas. While some locations might require a small fee, the convenience and coverage make it an excellent option for travelers who need reliable internet access.

5. Portable Wi-Fi Devices

If you're traveling with a group or require multiple devices to be connected, consider renting a portable Wi-Fi device. These pocket-sized devices provide a secure and private connection for your smartphones, tablets, and laptops. You can easily rent them at airports, or you might even be able to book them in advance online.

6. Wi-Fi Availability on Public Transportation

Taiwan's efficient public transportation system, including high-speed trains and metro systems, often provides free Wi-Fi onboard. This means you can catch up on emails, plan your itinerary, or simply enjoy some entertainment during your journeys.

7. Using Messaging Apps for Communication

Utilizing messaging apps like WhatsApp, LINE, and Facebook Messenger can be an economical way to stay connected with fellow travelers and locals.

Many Taiwanese use these apps for communication, making it convenient to connect with new friends or get local recommendations.

Whether you opt for a local SIM card, leverage the abundance of free Wi-Fi, or choose the flexibility of portable Wi-Fi devices, staying connected in Taiwan is a breeze. Having reliable access to the internet ensures you can navigate the country's treasures, share your experiences, and capture memories that will last a lifetime.

Chapter 18. Health and Safety

- *Travel Insurance*

When embarking on an exciting adventure to Taiwan, it's important to consider all aspects of your trip, including unexpected events that may arise. That's where travel insurance comes into play — a safeguard that ensures your peace of mind throughout your exploration of this beautiful island nation.

Why Travel Insurance Matters

Travel insurance is your safety net against the unforeseen, providing financial protection and assistance when things don't go according to plan. While Taiwan is a relatively safe and welcoming destination, unforeseen circumstances such as flight cancellations, medical emergencies, lost baggage, or unexpected trip interruptions can occur anywhere. Having travel insurance minimizes the financial impact of these situations, allowing you to focus on enjoying your journey.

Medical Emergencies and Healthcare

While Taiwan boasts a well-developed healthcare system, it's important to have travel insurance that covers medical emergencies. In the event of unexpected illnesses or accidents, your insurance can cover medical expenses, hospital stays, and even medical evacuation if necessary. This is particularly important, as medical costs can quickly escalate, and having insurance ensures you receive the care you need without incurring a heavy financial burden.

Trip Cancellations and Delays

Flight delays, cancellations, or trip interruptions can disrupt even the most carefully planned itineraries. Travel insurance can reimburse you for non-refundable expenses such as flights, accommodations, and tour bookings in case your plans are disrupted due to unforeseen circumstances like severe weather, strikes, or personal emergencies.

Lost Baggage and Personal Belongings

Losing your luggage or personal belongings can be a major inconvenience. Travel insurance can help cover the costs of replacing essential items, providing a safety net that allows you to continue your journey without major disruptions.

Coverage for Adventure Activities

If your Taiwan adventure includes adrenaline-pumping activities like hiking, water sports, or other adventure pursuits, make sure your travel insurance includes coverage for these activities. This can help ensure you're protected in case of accidents or injuries while participating in these endeavors.

How to Choose the Right Travel Insurance

When selecting a travel insurance plan for your trip to Taiwan, consider the following factors:

1. Coverage Limits: Ensure that the insurance coverage limits are adequate to cover potential expenses.

2. Medical Coverage: Check if the insurance covers medical expenses, hospitalization, and medical evacuation.

3. Cancellation Coverage: Confirm that the insurance covers trip cancellations, interruptions, and delays.

4. Adventure Activities: If you plan to engage in adventure activities, make sure they're covered by the policy.

5. Exclusions: Read the policy thoroughly to understand any exclusions or conditions that may affect your coverage.

6. Claim Process: Understand the process for filing claims and the necessary documentation.

7. Customer Support: Choose an insurance provider with 24/7 customer support for assistance during emergencies.

Travel insurance is an investment in the smooth and worry-free exploration of Taiwan. By securing the right coverage, you can focus on creating unforgettable memories and experiencing the beauty, culture, and adventure that Taiwan has to offer, knowing that you're protected in case the unexpected happens. Remember, while you may not anticipate needing it, travel insurance can provide invaluable support and peace of mind throughout your journey.

- *Medical Facilities and Pharmacies*

Ensuring your health and well-being while traveling is of utmost importance, and Taiwan boasts a robust healthcare system that provides both locals and visitors with high-quality medical services. Whether you're in need of medical attention or simply require over-the-counter remedies, you can rest assured that Taiwan has you covered.

Modern Healthcare Infrastructure

Taiwan is renowned for its advanced medical facilities and skilled healthcare professionals. The country's hospitals are equipped with state-of-the-art technology and adhere to international standards of care. Many doctors and medical staff are proficient in English, making communication seamless and easing any potential concerns.

Accessible Medical Services

In the event of a medical emergency, Taiwan's emergency response system is highly efficient. The number to call for emergency medical services is 119, and operators are trained to handle various situations, dispatching ambulances and medical personnel promptly. For non-emergencies, you can easily visit local clinics and hospitals.

Pharmacies and Medications

Pharmacies are readily available throughout Taiwan's cities and towns. They are typically denoted by a green cross sign and are easily recognizable. These establishments offer a range of over-the-counter medications, including pain relievers, cold and flu remedies, digestive aids, and more. Pharmacists are knowledgeable and can provide advice on selecting the right medication.

Prescription Medications

If you're traveling with prescription medications, it's advisable to carry a copy of your prescription, along with the generic names of the medications. In Taiwan, prescriptions from foreign doctors might not be recognized, but local physicians can provide equivalent medications based on the information you provide. It's recommended to consult with a local doctor to ensure you receive the appropriate treatment.

Health Insurance and Payment

Taiwan has a national health insurance system that provides coverage for both residents and tourists. However, it's important to check with your insurance provider to understand the extent of coverage during your stay in Taiwan. Keep in mind that you may need to pay for medical services upfront and then seek reimbursement from your insurance company later.

Traveler's Health Precautions

Taiwan is generally a safe destination health-wise, with good hygiene standards. However, it's advisable to take standard precautions, such as washing your hands regularly, staying hydrated, and consuming food from reputable sources. If you have specific health concerns or conditions, consulting with your healthcare provider before your trip is recommended.

Language Considerations

While many medical professionals in Taiwan speak English, it's always helpful to have essential medical phrases and terms translated into Chinese. This can aid communication, especially if you need to explain symptoms or conditions.

Taiwan's well-developed medical facilities, accessible pharmacies, and trained medical personnel contribute to a safe and secure travel experience. With a blend of modern healthcare infrastructure and a commitment to visitor well-being, Taiwan ensures that your health concerns are met with professionalism and efficiency, allowing you to explore the country with peace of mind.

- Emergency Contacts

Ensuring your safety and well-being during your travels is paramount, and familiarizing yourself with emergency contacts is a crucial part of any trip. Taiwan's efficient emergency response system is designed to provide quick assistance in times of need. Whether you're facing a medical situation, require police assistance, or need to report any issue, here are the essential emergency contacts to keep in mind during your time in Taiwan:

1. Police Emergency Line: 110

   In case of any criminal activity, accidents, or immediate threats to your safety, dial 110 to reach the local police. The police in Taiwan are generally responsive and can provide assistance in English as well as Mandarin.

2. Medical Emergencies: 119

For medical emergencies, including injuries, illnesses, or any urgent medical assistance, dial 119 to connect with an ambulance service. The medical staff is well-trained, and many hospitals in Taiwan have English-speaking personnel to aid communication.

3. Fire and Rescue: 119

If you encounter a fire, hazardous situation, or require rescue assistance, dial 119 to reach the fire department. They are equipped to handle various emergencies, from fires to natural disasters.

4. Taiwan Tourism Bureau's Tourist Hotline: 0800-011-765

This toll-free hotline is available for tourists seeking information, assistance, or reporting any issues. The operators can provide guidance in multiple languages and help connect you with the appropriate authorities.

5. Foreign Affairs Police: +886 2 2556 6001

If you encounter any issues related to immigration, visas, or other foreign affairs matters, you can contact the Foreign Affairs Police. They can provide guidance and support for travelers.

6. Local Embassy or Consulate

It's advisable to have the contact information of your country's embassy or consulate in Taiwan. They can offer assistance in case of emergencies, such as lost passports or other travel-related issues.

Remember to keep your phone charged and accessible at all times, and consider saving these emergency numbers in your contacts for quick access. In Taiwan, emergency services are generally efficient and reliable, ensuring that you'll receive the necessary help when needed. However, it's always a good idea to have travel insurance that covers medical emergencies and unexpected situations to ensure a worry-free journey.

As you explore Taiwan's vibrant cities, serene landscapes, and cultural wonders, knowing that you have access to these emergency contacts will contribute to a sense of security and confidence throughout your trip.

Chapter 19. Language Basics

- *Useful Phrases and Expressions*

As you embark on your journey through Taiwan, engaging with the local culture and people becomes a rewarding part of the experience. While English is widely spoken in tourist areas, making an effort to communicate in the local language can create meaningful connections and enhance your interactions. Here are some useful phrases and expressions to help you navigate your way through Taiwan:

Basic Greetings:
- Hello: 你好 (nǐ hǎo)
- Goodbye: 再見 (zàijiàn)
- Thank you: 謝謝 (xièxiè)
- Please: 請 (qǐng)
- Excuse me: 不好意思 (bù hǎoyìsi)
- Yes: 是 (shì)
- No: 不是 (bù shì)

Polite Phrases:
- I'm sorry: 對不起 (duìbùqǐ)
- You're welcome: 不客氣 (bù kèqì)
- May I ask...?: 請問 (qǐng wèn)
- Can you help me?: 你能幫我嗎？ (nǐ néng bāng wǒ ma?)

- I don't understand: 我不懂 (wǒ bù dǒng)

Getting Around:
- Where is...?: ...在哪裡？(...zài nǎlǐ?)
- How much is this?: 這個多少錢？(zhège duōshǎo qián?)
- I want to go to...: 我想去... (wǒ xiǎng qù...)
- Bus station: 公車站 (gōngchē zhàn)
- Train station: 火車站 (huǒchē zhàn)
- Airport: 機場 (jīchǎng)

Dining and Food:
- Menu: 菜單 (càidān)
- Water: 水 (shuǐ)
- Food: 食物 (shíwù)
- Delicious: 好吃 (hǎochī)
- I'm a vegetarian: 我吃素 (wǒ chī sù)

Shopping:
- How much does this cost?: 這個多少錢？(zhège duōshǎo qián?)
- Can you give me a discount?: 可以打個折嗎？(kěyǐ dǎgè zhé ma?)
- I'll take it: 我要這個 (wǒ yào zhège)
- Do you have...?: 有...嗎？(yǒu... ma?)

Emergency Situations:
- Help!: 幫幫我！(bāng bāng wǒ!)

- I need a doctor: 我需要看醫生 (wǒ xūyào kàn yīshēng)
- Police: 警察 (jǐngchá)

Cultural Courtesy:
- Taking photos: 可以拍照嗎？ (kěyǐ pāizhào ma?)
- Is this seat taken?: 這個座位有人嗎？ (zhège zuòwèi yǒurén ma?)

Making Friends:
- What's your name?: 你叫什麼名字？ (nǐ jiào shénme míngzì?)
- I'm from...: 我來自... (wǒ láizì...)
- Nice to meet you: 很高興認識你 (hěn gāoxìng rèn chí nǐ)

Navigating the Language Barrier:
- Do you speak English?: 你會說英文嗎？ (nǐ huì shuō Yīngwén ma?)
- Can you write that down?: 可以寫下來嗎？ (kěyǐ xiě xià lái ma?)

Embracing these phrases will not only assist you in practical situations but also show your genuine interest in engaging with the local culture. The Taiwanese people are incredibly welcoming, and your efforts to connect through language will undoubtedly lead to enriching encounters and a more immersive travel experience.

Chapter 20. Itinerary Suggestions

-Must-See Places

Taiwan is a treasure trove of captivating destinations that cater to every type of traveler. From bustling cities to serene countryside, the island offers a diverse range of experiences that will leave you awe-inspired. Here are some of the must-see places that should be on every traveler's itinerary:

1. Taipei: The dynamic capital city is a vibrant mix of modernity and tradition. Don't miss the iconic Taipei 101, once the world's tallest building, which offers breathtaking views of the city. Immerse yourself in the energy of bustling night markets like Shilin and Raohe, where you can sample mouthwatering local delicacies.

2. Taroko Gorge: Nature's masterpiece, Taroko Gorge is a stunning marble-walled canyon that offers breathtaking hiking trails and awe-inspiring vistas. The Swallow Grotto Trail and Baiyang Waterfall Trail are highlights, showcasing Taiwan's natural beauty.

3. Sun Moon Lake: This tranquil alpine lake surrounded by lush mountains is a romantic haven.

Take a boat cruise on the lake and visit the Ci'en Pagoda for panoramic views. The area is also known for its indigenous culture, adding a unique dimension to your visit.

4. Alishan National Scenic Area: Famous for its sunrise and sea of clouds, Alishan is a mountainous wonderland. The Alishan Forest Railway is a nostalgic journey through lush landscapes, while hiking trails offer a chance to connect with nature.

5. Kenting National Park: If you're a beach lover, Kenting is your paradise. With stunning beaches, coral reefs, and lush vegetation, it's a perfect spot for water sports, relaxation, and exploring the unique geological formations.

6. Tainan: As Taiwan's oldest city, Tainan is a cultural gem. Ancient temples like Koxinga Shrine and Anping Old Fort showcase the island's history. The bustling night markets and mouth watering local street food make Tainan a foodie's delight.

7. Jiufen: This charming mountain town is like stepping into a different era. Its narrow alleys, tea houses, and stunning views of the ocean create an atmosphere that has inspired artists and filmmakers.

8. Penghu Islands: Known for their turquoise waters, white sandy beaches, and unique basalt formations, the Penghu Islands are a paradise for beach lovers, water sports enthusiasts, and those seeking tranquility.

9. Lukang Historic Area: This small town is a living museum of traditional Taiwanese architecture and culture. Its well-preserved temples, narrow streets, and historic sites provide insight into Taiwan's past.

10. Yangmingshan National Park: Just a short drive from Taipei, this park offers diverse landscapes including hot springs, volcanic formations, and lush forests. The flower-filled meadows during spring and summer add to its charm.

11. Green Island: A volcanic island off Taiwan's eastern coast, Green Island offers clear waters perfect for snorkeling and diving. Explore the island's history at the former political prison and enjoy its relaxed atmosphere.

12. Lanyu (Orchid Island): Another island gem, Lanyu is home to the Tao indigenous people. Immerse yourself in their unique culture, enjoy

stunning coastal scenery, and discover traditional fishing practices.

These are just a few of the many captivating places Taiwan has to offer. Whether you're a solo traveler, a family with kids, a couple seeking romance, or anyone looking for adventure, Taiwan's must-see destinations will leave an indelible mark on your travel memories.

-7 Days in Taiwan

Welcome to your 7-day adventure through Taiwan! This itinerary has been carefully crafted to provide you with a perfect blend of urban exploration, natural beauty, cultural experiences, and delicious cuisine. From bustling cities to serene landscapes, get ready to immerse yourself in the heart of Taiwan's diverse offerings.

Day 1: Arrival in Taipei
- Arrive in Taipei, Taiwan's vibrant capital.
- Check into your hotel and freshen up.
- Explore the bustling streets of Ximending, known for shopping and street food.
- Visit Taipei 101, an iconic skyscraper with panoramic views.
- Enjoy a traditional Taiwanese dinner at a local eatery.

Day 2: Taipei Exploration
- Start your day with a visit to Chiang Kai-shek Memorial Hall and learn about Taiwan's history.
- Explore the National Palace Museum, home to an exquisite collection of Chinese art.
- Lunch at Din Tai Fung for renowned xiaolongbao (soup dumplings).
- Stroll through Daan Forest Park or visit the Shilin Night Market.
- Experience the lively atmosphere of Raohe Night Market and savor local snacks.

Day 3: Jiufen and Northern Coast
- Head to Jiufen, a charming mountain town with narrow alleys and tea houses.
- Enjoy panoramic views at Keelung's Miaokou Night Market.
- Discover Yehliu Geopark's fascinating rock formations.
- Return to Taipei for another delightful evening of city exploration.

Day 4: Taroko Gorge Excursion
- Take an early train to Hualien and embark on a day trip to Taroko Gorge.
- Marvel at the stunning marble cliffs, picturesque trails, and Baiyang Waterfall.

- Return to Hualien for dinner and relaxation.

Day 5: Sun Moon Lake
- Travel to Sun Moon Lake, a tranquil highland lake.
- Explore the lake's surroundings, including Wenwu Temple and Ci'en Pagoda.
- Enjoy a boat ride on the lake and take in the serene beauty.
- Overnight stay at Sun Moon Lake.

Day 6: Alishan National Scenic Area
- Depart for Alishan and witness the sunrise from the mountaintop.
- Explore Alishan's mystical forests, ancient trees, and scenic railway.
- Visit a tea plantation and learn about Taiwan's tea culture.
- Return to Taipei and indulge in a farewell dinner.

Day 7: Departure
- Depending on your flight time, you might have some free time for last-minute shopping or sightseeing.
- Check out from your hotel and head to the airport for your departure.

This 7-day Taiwan itinerary encapsulates the essence of the island's diverse offerings. From the bustling streets of Taipei to the natural wonders of Taroko Gorge and the tranquility of Sun Moon Lake and Alishan, you'll experience the cultural richness, breathtaking landscapes, and warm hospitality that Taiwan has to offer. Adjustments can be made based on your interests and travel pace, ensuring a memorable journey tailored to your preferences.

-10 Days of Adventure and Culture

Are you ready for an unforgettable journey that combines thrilling outdoor escapades with deep cultural immersions? This 10-day adventure and culture itinerary in Taiwan is meticulously crafted to provide you with an immersive experience of the island's natural beauty, rich history, and vibrant traditions.

Day 1-2: Taipei - Gateway to Taiwan

Day 1: Arrival in Taipei
- Arrive in Taipei and check into your hotel.
- Explore the bustling streets of Ximending, known for its shopping and entertainment.
- Enjoy a flavorful Taiwanese dinner at a local eatery.

Day 2: Taipei Exploration
- Visit the Chiang Kai-shek Memorial Hall and learn about Taiwan's history.
- Explore the National Palace Museum, home to a vast collection of Chinese artifacts.
- Wander through the historic streets of Dadaocheng and indulge in some nostalgic charm.
- Delight in a night market feast at Shilin Night Market, savoring various street food delicacies.

Day 3-4: Taroko Gorge - Nature's Masterpiece

Day 3: Travel to Hualien
- Take a scenic train ride to Hualien.
- Check into your accommodation and relax amidst nature.

Day 4: Taroko Gorge Adventure
- Embark on a breathtaking day trip to Taroko Gorge, hiking its stunning trails.
- Visit the Baiyang Waterfall Trail and the Eternal Spring Shrine.
- Immerse yourself in the awe-inspiring marble-walled canyons.

Day 5-6: Taitung - Coastal Beauty and Indigenous Culture

Day 5: Journey to Taitung
- Travel to Taitung, a coastal gem known for its indigenous culture.
- Visit the Taitung Seashore Park and unwind by the ocean.

Day 6: Indigenous Experiences
- Explore the Beinan Cultural Park, showcasing Taiwan's indigenous heritage.
- Discover traditional crafts, music, and dance.
- Relax at a local hot spring, rejuvenating body and soul.

Day 7-8: Kenting National Park - Sun, Sand, and Adventure

Day 7: Arrival in Kenting
- Reach Kenting National Park, a haven for outdoor enthusiasts.
- Settle in your accommodation and savor the coastal atmosphere.

Day 8: Outdoor Adventures
- Enjoy water activities like snorkeling or diving in the crystal-clear waters.
- Hike the trails of Maobitou Park for panoramic views.

- Explore Kenting's lively night market and indulge in fresh seafood.

Day 9-10: Kaohsiung - Urban Vibes and Cultural Treasures

Day 9: Exploring Kaohsiung
- Arrive in Kaohsiung, Taiwan's second-largest city.
- Visit the Lotus Pond and admire its vibrant temples.
- Take a stroll along the Love River and enjoy the city's modern ambiance.

Day 10: Cultural Immersion
- Discover the Fo Guang Shan Monastery, a renowned Buddhist center.
- Explore the Pier-2 Art Center, an artistic hub in the city.
- Conclude your journey with a scenic sunset view from Sizihwan Bay.

This 10-day adventure and culture itinerary in Taiwan takes you on a mesmerizing journey from the vibrant streets of Taipei to the natural wonders of Taroko Gorge, the indigenous traditions in Taitung, the coastal beauty of Kenting, and the urban charm of Kaohsiung. Immerse yourself in

Taiwan's diverse landscapes, rich history, and warm hospitality as you create memories to last a lifetime. Whether you're seeking outdoor thrills or cultural insights, Taiwan promises an unforgettable experience.

-5-Day Romantic Retreat

Are you seeking a romantic escape that combines breathtaking landscapes, intimate experiences, and moments of shared wonder? Taiwan, with its diverse offerings of natural beauty, charming towns, and luxurious hideaways, provides the perfect setting for a memorable 5-day romantic retreat. Whether you're celebrating an anniversary, embarking on a honeymoon, or simply nurturing your bond, this itinerary promises to create cherished memories that will linger for a lifetime.

Day 1: Taipei - A Romantic Urban Adventure
- Morning: Begin your journey in Taipei, Taiwan's vibrant capital. Start with a leisurely stroll through Da'an Forest Park, a lush oasis in the heart of the city, ideal for a peaceful morning walk hand in hand.
- Afternoon: Head to the iconic Taipei 101 skyscraper. Ascend to the observatory for panoramic views, especially mesmerizing during

sunset. Share a romantic dinner at a rooftop restaurant nearby.
- Evening: Explore the bustling Shilin Night Market, where you can try local delicacies while soaking in the lively atmosphere.

Day 2: Sun Moon Lake - Serene Waters and Tranquil Moments
- Morning: Travel to Sun Moon Lake, a picturesque gem known for its breathtaking landscapes. Enjoy a sunrise boat ride, watching the lake and mountains come to life with the morning light.
- Afternoon: Take a leisurely bike ride or a scenic walk around the lake's perimeter, stopping to visit quaint villages and lakeside temples.
- Evening: Dine at a lakeside restaurant, savoring a delicious meal while being surrounded by the calming presence of the lake.

Day 3: Alishan National Scenic Area - Whispering Forests and Starry Skies
- Morning: Journey to Alishan and explore the mystical Alishan Forest Recreation Area. Stroll hand in hand through the towering cypress trees, creating an ethereal atmosphere.
- Afternoon: Discover the enchanting Sister Ponds, offering serene reflections. Enjoy a tranquil picnic in this serene setting.

- Evening: Stay overnight in Alishan and, weather permitting, witness the mesmerizing sea of clouds during sunrise. Wrap up the day with stargazing, as Alishan offers some of the best views of the night sky.

Day 4: Jiufen and Jinguashi - A Journey Through Time
- Morning: Travel to Jiufen, a charming village known for its narrow alleys, historic architecture, and stunning coastal views. Explore the alleys hand in hand, discovering quaint tea houses and artisan shops.
- Afternoon: Head to Jinguashi to visit the Gold Ecological Park. Take a guided tour to learn about the region's mining history and enjoy the scenic views.
- Evening: Return to Jiufen in the evening to witness the town's magical transformation as lanterns illuminate its streets.

Day 5: Beitou - Relaxation and Rejuvenation
- Morning: Travel to Beitou, a hot spring haven near Taipei. Soak in a private outdoor hot spring bath at a luxurious spa resort, surrounded by lush greenery.

- Afternoon: Enjoy a couple's massage or spa treatment, followed by a leisurely walk through Beitou's Thermal Valley.
- Evening: Conclude your romantic retreat with a quiet dinner at a Beitou restaurant, basking in the warmth of shared moments and the rejuvenation of body and spirit.

As your 5-day romantic retreat in Taiwan comes to an end, you'll carry with you a collection of cherished memories and a deepened connection with your loved one, all woven through the tapestry of Taiwan's diverse landscapes, rich culture, and warm hospitality.

-Family-Focused 14-Day Adventure

Traveling with your family offers a unique opportunity to create cherished memories and deepen your bonds. Taiwan, with its family-friendly attractions, scenic landscapes, and warm hospitality, is an ideal destination for such an adventure. This 14-day itinerary ensures a well-balanced mix of fun activities, cultural exploration, and relaxation for families of all sizes.

Day 1-3: Taipei - The Capital Start
- Day 1: Arrive in Taipei, settle into your family-friendly accommodation, and take a

leisurely stroll around Ximending, a vibrant shopping district.
- Day 2: Visit the National Palace Museum, where the kids can marvel at ancient artifacts, and then explore the interactive exhibits at the Taipei Children's Amusement Park.
- Day 3: Discover the Taipei Zoo, home to pandas and a diverse range of animals. Conclude the day with a visit to Taipei 101 for panoramic city views.

Day 4-5: Northern Charms
- Day 4: Head to Jiufen, an enchanting town with narrow lanes and teahouses. Let your kids indulge in some taro or sweet potato ice cream.
- Day 5: Explore Yehliu Geopark's fascinating rock formations and have a relaxing time at Fulong Beach, building sandcastles and enjoying the sea.

Day 6-7: Eastern Wonders
- Day 6: Journey to Hualien and explore Taroko Gorge National Park. Hike the family-friendly trails and be amazed by the stunning marble scenery.
- Day 7: Visit Farglory Ocean Park for amusement rides, a water park, and animal exhibits that will delight the entire family.

Day 8-10: Central Adventures

- Day 8: Travel to Taichung and explore the
Rainbow Village, a colorful art-filled community.
- Day 9: Spend the day at the Formosan Aboriginal
Culture Village, a theme park that offers insights
into indigenous culture and fun rides.
- Day 10: Discover Sun Moon Lake, enjoy a boat
ride, and take a cable car ride for breathtaking
views.

Day 11-13: Southern Escapades
- Day 11: Head to Tainan, explore Anping Old
Street, and take a rickshaw ride around historic
sites.
- Day 12: Visit the Ten Drum Culture Village for a
unique drumming experience and enjoy the
kid-friendly attractions.
- Day 13: Relax at Kenting National Park, where
your family can enjoy beaches, nature walks, and
water sports.

Day 14: Farewell Taipei
- Day 14: Return to Taipei. Spend your last day
shopping for souvenirs at Shilin Night Market,
savoring local treats one last time.

This 14-day family-focused adventure provides a
blend of excitement and relaxation, ensuring that
every member of your family will have a memorable

time exploring Taiwan's diverse attractions. Be it the bustling cities, serene landscapes, or engaging cultural experiences, this itinerary offers a well-rounded family journey that you'll treasure forever.

The Legend of Formosus and the Jade Island

Long ago, in the heart of the East China Sea, lay a lush and beautiful island known as Formosa. Its forests were dense, its mountains majestic, and its waters teemed with life. But above all, it was the island's history that captivated the hearts of those who called it home.

In the village of Yilan, nestled between the emerald mountains and the azure coast, lived a young fisherman named Formosus. He was known for his courage and kindness, always willing to help his fellow villagers in times of need. One day, as he cast his net into the sea, he caught something that shimmered like a thousand stars.

To his amazement, Formosus pulled up a small jade pendant, intricate in design and radiating an otherworldly light. The village elders recognized it as a gift from the sea gods, a symbol of protection and prosperity. As time passed, Formosus' village thrived, their nets full of fish and their hearts full of gratitude.

However, Formosus' act of kindness did not go unnoticed by the sea spirits. One moonlit night, a figure emerged from the waves, her hair flowing like seaweed and her eyes gleaming like pearls. She introduced herself as Lirael, the guardian spirit of the East China Sea. In gratitude for his selflessness, Lirael offered Formosus a choice—a single wish, to be granted at a moment of his choosing.

Formosus, humbled by the spirit's offer, asked for the well-being of his people and the eternal preservation of Formosa's natural beauty. Lirael granted his wish, and in doing so, she transformed the island into a sanctuary of lush forests, towering mountains, and crystal-clear waters. The creatures of the land and sea coexisted harmoniously, and Formosa became a haven of tranquility and wonder.

As the years passed, Formosus' story became a legend whispered by the island's inhabitants. It spoke of the interconnectedness between humanity and nature, the importance of selflessness, and the enduring beauty of Formosa. Visitors from near and far would hear this tale and be inspired by the island's history—a history that is etched into the very soul of Taiwan.

And so, as you leave Formosa, take with you not just memories of vibrant night markets, breathtaking landscapes, and intricate temples, but also the legend of Formosus and the Jade Island.

For in this tale, you will find the essence of Taiwan—the spirit of a land where kindness, harmony, and the bond between humans and nature continue to thrive, just as they did in the days of old.

Made in United States
Troutdale, OR
09/07/2023

12708437R00139